The
Once-a-Week
Cooking Plan

The Incredible Cooking Program That Will
Save You 10 to 20 Hours a Week
(and Have Your Family Begging for More!)

JONI HILTON

Prima Publishing

PRIMA PUBLISHING and colophon are registered trademarks of Prima Communications, Inc.

Interior illustrations by Sheryl Dickert

Interior design by The Salmon Studio

Library of Congress Cataloging-in-Publication Data

Hilton, Joni.
  The once-a-week cooking plan : the incredible cooking program that will save you 10-20 hours a week (and have your family begging for more!) / Joni Hilton.
      p.   cm.
  Includes index.
  ISBN 0-7615-1773-1
  1. Make-ahead cookery. I. Title.
  TX652.H647   1998
  641.5'55—dc21   98-32311
                                          CIP

99 00 01 02 03 DD 10 9 8 7 6 5 4 3 2 1
Printed in the United States of America

How to Order

Single copies may be ordered from Prima Publishing, P.O. Box 1260BK, Rocklin, CA 95677; telephone (916) 632-4400. Quantity discounts are also available. On your letterhead, include information concerning the intended use of the books and the number of books you wish to purchase.

Visit us online at www.primalifestyles.com

To my husband, Bob, and our children,
Richie, Brandon, Cassidy, and Nicole.
I love you more than cookie dough.

CONTENTS

Contents   *vii*

Have you ever noticed that when you run across a really great idea, you think, "Why hasn't anybody thought of this before?" Certain ideas are so obviously wonderful—and make life so simple—that we use them right away, and only wish we'd heard about them sooner.

Cooking once a week is one of those brilliant ideas. It makes life so much easier, you'll honestly wonder why you knocked yourself out shopping and cooking and cleaning the old-fashioned way. *You will love it!*

How Once-a-Week Cooking Works

This method allows you to shop just once a week, instead of popping into the grocery store whenever you remember you need something. Each chapter (starting with chapter seven) lists the meals you will prepare for that week, providing a user-friendly format and the same four, easy elements to help you prepare them.

MENU

The menu is a list of all the recipes for each week. The menus vary, but each one will contain at least two of the following groups according to food type:

> Soup
> Salad
> Main Dishes
> Side Dishes
> Dessert

Some menus may not contain every group, but each menu contains five delicious main dishes and at least one dessert, and gives you a brief overview of what delicious things you and your family will have to look forward to that week.

SHOPPING LIST

I've compiled easy shopping lists for you. You'll probably already have many of the basics on hand in your kitchen, and you'll only need to pick up a few things. Each list provides the exact measurement of each item you'll need when you prepare your meals. This way, you'll know exactly what you need to buy at the grocery store, depending on what you already have.

PUTTING IT ALL TOGETHER

For each week, I've included a page called "Putting It All Together." This is a numbered list of every task you'll need to complete before assembling the meals. Block out two to three hours of time—choose a Saturday morning, a Wednesday night, whatever is best for you. It works best for me to take a few minutes to cook up *all* the onions, for example, and grate *all* the cheese for that week. We've always been taught to put everything away as we cook, but—with apologies to all the cooks of yesteryear—we're going to change that. It makes far more sense to do everything you can with the flour or pepper before you put it back on the shelf. You'll save steps, believe me. Then you can do a big cleanup after your two or three hours of cooking.

FROM PANTRY TO PLATE

After you put your ingredients together, follow the step-by-step instructions in this section to make a week's worth of meals at once. Even non-cooks can do this—I've kept every recipe deliberately simple. Cooking once a week works for families with kids, for single parents, for big families, for adults living alone or in shared households, for homeschooling families, for child-free couples—just about everybody!

You'll be amazed at how quickly the dishes come together—while the rice is cooking for one dish, you can thaw vegetables for another, and sprinkle on the pizza toppings for yet another. Instead of taking five hours to make five dinners, you'll overlap the preparations and cut the time in half! Then you wrap, label, and freeze everything.

Now the fun begins. Each evening, you (or whoever gets home first) pulls out that day's dinner. No thinking, no sighing, no washing a bunch of pots. Pop dinner in the oven, and the next thing you know, you're sitting down to a delicious, nutritious—and economical—meal. Isn't this the life you've always wanted?

TIP:

When considering making an elaborate dish, don't shy away from recipes that have many steps. Make several servings at once and freeze them. Then you can enjoy the dish again without having to repeat all the steps.

We're beginning a new century, and it's time we stopped cooking the way we did a hundred years ago. *The Once-a-Week Cooking Plan* will revolutionize the way you think about and practice cooking. This new method is so much quicker, so much more nutritious, and—if I do say so myself—better for the soul. It reduces stress and gives you more family or personal time. You will automatically become more organized. And it's fun!

We're all so busy that many people have resorted to microwaving everything, and the art of good cooking has gotten lost. This book will show you how to reach both goals—quick fixing *and* good eating. I don't expect that most people will want to cook more than five meals a week, but for those who really do cook seven days a week, this plan will be an even bigger relief. For the extra two days, refer to chapter 4, which describes basic mixes and gives you dozens of recipes to make with them. I cannot overstate the value of keeping some of these basic mixes in the freezer; they will simplify your life again and again. Use them for an entire week if you wish.

Let me give you six great reasons to switch to once-a-week cooking:

Money

You will be astounded at how economical it is to cook a week's worth of meals all at one time. You'll start buying in bulk, even if you're a household of one. You'll discover ways to use the same item in several dishes, instead of investing in a bunch of exotic ingredients that only get half-used and then sit in the back of the refrigerator until they look like a row of Chia pets. And, if you're like many people, you've been resorting to fast food a few nights a week. Cutting out those trips means the money you once spent will now stay in your pocket. And you thought this method was just about saving time!

Time

This is where weekly cooking really pays off. You are on the brink of becoming an entirely new person—one whose kids actually recognize as a familiar face . . . somebody they look in the eye, talk to, laugh with, and even beat at Monopoly more often than not. A happy person who suddenly has delicious chunks of time to invest in the family.

Be ready for the holidays. Make cookies, candies, and muffins ahead of time, and freeze them in rigid containers. You'll show up with all these wondrous homemade goodies, and friends will simply marvel and wonder how you do it!

It's so easy just to pull something homemade out of the freezer. You don't have to add anything to these prepared-in-advance meals unless you want to. While the main elements are warming up, you can quickly prepare a salad or dessert.

And, when holidays roll around, since you won't be worn out from constant daily cooking, you might actually *want* to make that bread dough cornucopia. You'll have more energy for creating dishes from your heritage or rolls made from scratch—the traditions people love and remember.

Sanity

You know how hard it is sometimes to complete a thought without getting interrupted? Kiss those days goodbye. With cooking once a week, you'll now have so much mental energy you'll finish your thoughts and even get to those unfinished projects you've been putting on the back burner. What a kick, to be able to make dinner without depleting your last reserves of creativity. I have a friend who says, "After a full day at the office, if I'm going to have any energy left for my family, dinner has to be a no-brainer." Once-a-week cooking is the ultimate way to give your brain a rest at least five days out of seven.

Good Food

I love creating yummy dishes. Even as I'm eating something, I'm thinking, "What if we added citrus to this?" or "What if this were stacked vertically?" "What if crushed basil were stirred into this dough?" Yes, I like the basics, but I also love "to die for" desserts, innovative sauces, and gourmet treats. So you'll not only save time, money, and sanity with this book—you'll garner a reputation as a fabulous cook. These recipes are delicious, and even if you never freeze a single one, you'll be eating wonderful meals and marveling at how easy it was to whip them up. That's one of the reasons I win so many recipe contests: I know how to keep it simple, so that even non-cooks can prepare sensational meals in only minutes. (My award-winning recipes now belong to the sponsors of those cook-offs, but I've included some variations that are just as tasty.)

You'll find that the recipes in this book are flexible. If cayenne pepper is too strong for you, leave it out. Add some oregano or garlic. You can spice these recipes up or down, or substitute your favorite ingredients for ones that don't suit your taste or budget. Use chicken instead of shrimp, lemon instead of lime. Cooking is most fun when it's creative. If you'd rather use a canned cream soup instead of a white sauce, make life easy on yourself and do it.

Teamwork

Once-a-week cooking makes it a snap for the whole household to pitch in and get dinner started. Whoever comes home first can pop that night's dinner into the oven, and by the time everyone has dropped their backpacks and briefcases, a steaming, fragrant dinner is waiting.

Others can even pitch in on cooking day as part of the assembly line. (See chapter 5, on how to involve children in cooking.) Computer whizzes can help by making adhesive labels for the food you're freezing.

Reduced Cleanup

Think of the time and trouble you'll save cleaning up once a week, instead of daily. Why should we scrub pans and spatulas every night?

Think of it the way you do laundry: Would you run a load of wash each night, just to launder what you wore each day? Of course not. Instead, you do things sensibly: You put dirty clothes in the hamper until you have a full load.

Before the invention of refrigerators, people had to shop for food every day. Now that there are freezers, we can cook once a week and do our cleanup then, too. There are no pots to scrub each day, no mixing bowls to wash. The only cleanup you'll have are each day's plates, glasses, and silverware. Rinse them and load the dishwasher or sink, wipe down the counters—two minutes instead of twenty. (And if you occasionally use paper plates and plastic utensils, you won't even have to wash up.) Now let's get started.

TIP:

Cool down spicy foods for those who don't like the heat: Stir in sour cream or sugar

The Once-a-Week Cooking Plan

shopping strategies

When you follow the once-a-week cooking plan, you'll not only save time on daily food preparation and cleanup, you'll save time shopping as well. Once a week, you'll buy everything you need for your one cooking day. Ask the grocery clerks when the store is the least busy, and try to shop then. Eliminate the days of running to the market because you need "something for dinner tonight."

Check out the big grocery warehouses. Sometimes you save money there, and sometimes you don't. If visiting a warehouse means you'll buy more than you need and break your budget, stick with the local supermarkets. But consider buying at least your staple items in bulk. Salt, flour, eggs, milk, yes. But the warehouse stores don't have as many choices for the items that bring your meals to life. (They might have ketchup, but they won't have tomato sauce with your favorite chilies in it.) And don't overlook the savings at smaller, bag-it-yourself stores.

I study trends in cooking, and the recipes in this book reflect that. There are so many exciting new products coming out all the time—terrific ethnic dishes, novel desserts. You'll enjoy cooking and eating much more if you experiment from time to time. This doesn't mean you'll get so exotic that your family or guests won't recognize anything you've made; it just means you'll go beyond the "cream of mushroom soup" school of cooking to a level of taste that makes meals exciting and worth the effort you've put into them.

When shopping, remember to look for the freshest, best quality ingredients you can find. If you don't use the best ingredients, your final creations will be disappointing—what a waste of time,

Consider an even easier, though somewhat costlier way to simplify cooking: Precooked chicken strips and bacon. You can buy these at the market, all ready to heat and use in your favorite recipes. (You can even find flavored chicken strips—this saves several more cooking steps.) Be on the lookout for the ever-changing array of new convenience foods that'll make my easy recipes still easier.

and money, too. When I was in cooking school in France, they told a story about a man named Paul Bocuse: He was begging his grandmother on her deathbed for a secret recipe. All his life he wanted to know why her potatoes were so delicious, and she finally told him. "First," she said, "Go dig up the potatoes." The point of this story is freshness. To create wonderful food, you need to start with the highest quality you can find.

Now, surprisingly, the "freshest ingredients" doesn't always mean fresh vegetables from the produce department. From your garden, yes. But in the produce department, you don't know how long ago that corn was picked, or whether it's been stored in the hot sun. A broccoli grower once told me that frozen broccoli is actually your freshest bet, because it's flash-frozen right in the fields, whereas "fresh" broccoli might ride for hours in a truck before it's ready for sale. I often opt for frozen over "fresh" because I actually get higher quality. And if you're planning to freeze the meals you fix, starting with already cut, washed, frozen items really streamlines the work.

The first thing to do is to plan your week's menu from the selections in this book. Write down all the ingredients you'll need. Group them into categories, so that when you go to the market, you'll shop in a time-saving, efficient way. List all your dairy products together, all your cleaning supplies together, and so on. I fold a sheet of paper in half three times, which gives me eight sections to write in. I use each of these sections for a different category. Then, when I need to add tomatoes, paper towels, and multivitamins, I add them in the sections where they belong, instead of at the end of a list that will send me back where I've already been. Being organized isn't an inherited trait; it's a choice smart people make to give themselves more time.

You know the layout of your market, so list the items you'll purchase in the order that works best for you. In the shopping lists I've created for you, I've categorized generically because most markets are designed differently. For example, I use the following eight categories:

Cleaners (includes paper goods and health items)
Canned goods
Rice/pasta

TIP:

Use canned yams and beets—these two vegetables taste the same fresh or canned!

Breads and cereals
Produce
Meats
Dairy and deli
Frozen foods

I try to buy in that order, so the perishable items will stay cold. Obviously, if you buy baby food or pet supplies, you'll need to add those to your list.

Watch for sales on items you frequently use, then stock up. Let's say you use lots of tortillas, not just for tacos, but for wraps, pizzas, nachos, lasagna, and sandwiches. When there's a sale on tortillas, you're wise to buy a dozen packages and keep them in the freezer. Smart shopping gives you the flexibility to buy in quantity when things you need are on sale, in addition to your running list of the things you need.

It also makes wonderful sense to freeze summer fruits so that you can enjoy them during the winter. Great taste, and great economics! Later in the book I'll show you some ways to do this. Of course, you don't want to take up so much freezer space on extras that you no longer have room for your week's meals. So experiment and see how much room you'll have. (If you really want to freeze that bumper crop of sweet corn, you might want to consider buying an extra freezer.) This book shows you how to make a week's worth of meals that will fit into the freezer space of a regular refrigerator. If you still have room left over, I think you'll find plenty of ways to fill it!

Buy already made crepes at the super-market, then keep them in the freezer. Thaw at room temperature and fill for a quick meal or dessert.

TIP:

If you have room in your freezer, buy extra milk and freeze it. Milk freezes just fine, and will come in handy if you suddenly run out.

freezing techniques

How much freezer space do you really need? We have four land sharks—I mean children—including two teenage boys, so with a family of six (plus the friends who frequently drop in for dinner) we find that two refrigerators placed side by side are perfect for us. We looked into commercial refrigerators, and found not only that two regular refrigerators were less expensive than one Big Mama fridge, but also that they actually gave us more cubic feet of freezer space. However, you can still freeze a week's worth of food in one refrigerator's freezer space. We just like lots of extras (like ice cream).

Keep your freezer temperature at o degrees F or lower. There's no sense freezing good food and then having it spoil because it wasn't kept cold enough. If your freezer is opened frequently its temperature may rise, so you might even consider keeping it at −10 degrees.

Also, to save on cooling costs, keep your freezer at least two-thirds full. A full freezer works much more economically than a nearly empty one. Use your extra space to freeze seasonal items, such as herbs and strawberries, and enjoy them months later. Don't forget that some of your space will probably be taken up storing ice, juice concentrates, and extra loaves of bread.

Containers

Freeze everything in square or rectangular containers only. One of my best friends is Deniece Schofield, author of *Confessions of an Organized Homemaker*, and *Kitchen Organization Tips and Secrets*. If anybody's an expert on saving space, it's Deniece. And she absolutely refuses to use round containers, not only in the

My husband and I finally found a way to hide the premium ice cream from the kids (who'll swallow anything, we've discovered, and can't yet tell good ice cream from the two-dollar-a-gallon kind). We wrapped the ice cream in a brown paper bag and labeled it "Raw Liver."

TIP:

Freeze meat in a
freezer bag with mari-
nade ingredients.
Then, as it thaws,
it marinates.

freezer, but in cupboards. They eat up valuable storage space, and they're harder to label, too. Flat-sided containers can be lined up and stacked much more efficiently.

You also want a container that's meant to be frozen. Not all round containers are intended for freezer use. Thin margarine tubs allow too much air and moisture leakage in freezers to ensure good quality and safety.

So what can you use? Foil compartment trays are great (remember TV dinners?) for dividing up meals into individual portions. But my freezer mostly contains plastic resealable freezer bags and square plastic containers with tight-fitting lids. The key to any freezer container is that it must be airtight and moisture proof.

When using plastic bags, be sure to squeeze out all the air you can. If the bags are not self-sealing, use twist ties or rubber bands to secure them. Recycle the bags when you're finished with them.

I like to freeze food in a container such as a bread loaf pan, or a plastic box with an airtight lid, then transfer the food to a resealable bag once it's frozen. This allows for efficient stacking in the freezer, and also frees up a baking or storing dish. (Or place your resealable bags in the loaf pan or plastic container so the bags will freeze in that shape). An even easier method is to use freezer-to-oven baking dishes, and leave the food in one container from start to finish. If you use baking dishes with lids, be sure to seal them with freezer tape.

By all means, take time to label your packages. Write directly on a disposable container, or on freezer tape or masking tape, with an indelible marker. Label the contents, the number of portions, and the date frozen, and include reheating instructions.

Some people like to use the foil pans with crimped sides, but I find these not only expensive, but maddening to clean. If you want to reuse these pans, I suggest lining them with sheets of foil.

Freezer wrap or heavy-duty foil are excellent choices. Place your food in the center of the wrap or foil, bring two sides up, and fold over until the food is tightly encased. Now fold the remaining sides of the wrapping material tightly into triangles and bring them up over the food, as if wrapping a gift. Tape securely.

When you've used the food wrapped this way, be sure to recycle the aluminum foil (as long as it stays clean).

When filling any container, leave room for expansion. This is called "head space." And whatever container you choose, keep the sealing edges clean. Much of your cooking and freezing will be in assembly-line fashion, and you'll want to make cleanliness a top priority.

Precautions

Freezing does not kill bacteria; it only stops its growth until the food thaws out again. Therefore, you'll want to freeze fresh food as quickly as possible. Remember, air is your enemy. This doesn't mean you pour boiling hot soup into a freezer bag and pop it into the freezer. If you load your freezer with too many hot foods at once, it might affect your freezer temperature. Instead, cool foods quickly before you freeze them. (Quickly does not mean cooling on the kitchen counter at room temperature; you could risk spoiling.)

If you have a power outage, don't open the freezer; everything inside should be OK for two days. This is another good reason to keep your freezer full; the more food you have in it, the longer it will take to thaw if power is interrupted. If food does begin to thaw, wrap it in newspaper—a great insulator—and use dry ice to keep it cold in the freezer. (Always wear gloves when handling dry ice, and don't let it come in direct contact with food—wrap the ice in paper.)

Thawing

When ready to thaw your meals, there are three ways to do so:

1. Thaw them in the refrigerator (never on the kitchen counter).
2. Set your container in a pot of warm water until the contents release from the container, then transfer the food to the top of a double boiler and cook it immediately.
3. Defrost food in the microwave oven.

The only exceptions to these thawing instructions are desserts; they can thaw at room temperature.

TIP:

To chill hot foods quickly, place them in containers, and then into a pan of ice water. Or, put them in the refrigerator until they're cool enough to handle. *Then* load them into the freezer.

You need to plan ahead when thawing; simply take out tomorrow's dinner and place it in the fridge tonight. For example, a chicken smaller than 4 pounds will take 12 to 16 hours to thaw in the refrigerator. More than 4 pounds might take a day to a day and a half.

What if you forget to thaw? If you realize the oversight soon enough, you can still cook something that's frozen; just divide the cooking time in half and add the resulting number to the cooking time. Or, switch to something that's frozen in smaller pieces: Instead of a roast, serve chopped barbecued beef. Or serve diced chicken tossed with a salad, instead of serving whole pieces. You can also change your cooking method: Stir-fry instead of bake, or broil instead of steam.

Casseroles can go directly from the freezer to the oven; they'll just need to bake longer when frozen than they would if you thawed them first. A frozen casserole can be covered and cooked at 400 degrees F for one hour. Then, uncover it and cook another 45 minutes.

It's OK to refreeze food, as long as it hasn't started to spoil. But remember, the quality of refrozen food will not be as high as when it was originally frozen, and many vegetables will turn mushy.

This book is designed to help you cook once a week, then use those meals during the following week. But what if you've prepared all the meals, and one night you spontaneously decide you want to go out to dinner? No problem. Everything in this book can be kept in the freezer for at least a month, and some items a year or more. Get enough dinner invitations and you can stockpile an entire week's worth of extra meals!

freezing foods

When you're planning to freeze what you cook, it's a good idea to keep the frozen meals fairly low in fat. Lower-fat meals will thaw better, because fat tends to separate after it's frozen. As you look over recipes you might want to try, it's fairly easy to see where you can cut back on fat. Use reduced-fat cream cheese, light sour cream or yogurt, fat-free sweetened condensed milk, nonfat milk, fat-free egg substitutes, reduced-fat baking mixes, lean cuts of meat instead of fatty ones, buttermilk in pastries, baking instead of frying, applesauce instead of half the oil in baked goods. Learn to season with herbs instead of oil. Your results after thawing will be better, and you'll be healthier for it. The one indulgence I never replace is butter, however, because I've never found the perfect substitute for its flavor. But if you're being "good" everywhere else, a little dab of butter isn't so bad, is it?

In chapters 7 through 20 I give you recipes for making and freezing a week's worth of meals. But it can be very time-efficient to freeze specific foods ahead of time and later work them into your week's cooking. Following are instructions for preparing and freezing these standard "time-savers."

Freezing Individual Foods
Use these easy guidelines again and again as you get into the habit of freezing food instead of trying to store everything in the refrigerator.

BUTTER
Butter simply keeps longer in the freezer than in the fridge. Wrap it tightly to seal in the flavor, then freeze the butter up to six months (if butter is salted), or up to ten months (if butter is unsalted).

TIP:
Freeze cheese in
blocks; it will be more
crumbly, but the flavor
will still be good.

SOUPS

Soups freeze wonderfully. However, they can take up a lot of freezer space. The solution is to concentrate them as much as possible, adding most of the liquid only when reheating. When you initially make soup, leave out as much liquid as possible. Your freezer label will read something like, "Vegetable Beef Soup, frozen January 15, serves 6, add 2 cans stewed tomatoes, 1 quart stock." When you reheat the soup, add the liquid ingredients, and voilà!

You can also freeze individual portions of soups. Use mugs, muffin tins, and small bowls. These are great for nights when you're alone, or when everybody's eating at a different time.

You can double the amount of soup by adding frozen, cooked pasta in the last few minutes of heating.

Creamy soups should be reheated in the top of a double boiler over simmering water. They may look curdled at first, but as you heat and stir them, they should smooth out.

Don't keep soups in the freezer for more than six months.

MEATS, POULTRY, AND FISH

Beef stew is terrific to freeze because it can be so versatile. If you make a huge batch and enjoy it the first night as stew, you can tuck the rest away in the freezer and bring it out a few days later in a completely "new" form. Add stock and pasta to make it a soup, cover it with pastry dough to make a pot pie, stir it into a noodle casserole, or even create a hearty quiche with it. If you want to have it as stew again, stir in a little cumin, curry, or Jamaican Jerk seasoning and give it an ethnic twist.

Ground beef is a common ingredient in most homes. As long as you're cooking some up, you may as well cook up several pounds and freeze it for later use. Stir in onions as well (use frozen chopped onions for greater ease) and frozen chopped mushrooms. As the beef thaws later, it will be even more flavorful. In chapter 4 I tell you exactly how to do this, and provide some suggestions for serving it various ways. (Two cups of cooked ground beef will be the equivalent of about a pound.)

Beef patties are easy, too. Freeze with waxed paper between them for easy separation. Meat loaf can be mixed up and frozen ahead of time. (My secret ingredient is leftover stuffing—it already has onions, celery, mushrooms, and sausage in it.) Individual meat

TIP:
Thaw fish in milk for
freshest taste.

The Once-a-Week Cookbook

loaves are a great idea—just defrost as many as you need instead of a whole loaf. They're quicker thawing and quicker baking. All these ground beef products will keep for about two months, so be sure to date your packages and rotate them.

When thawing larger cuts of meat that will need to be sliced, cut them before they thaw completely; partially frozen meat is much easier to slice. And if you're leaving the meat whole, re-member to allow more time to cook a frozen roast as a refrig-erated one.

To freeze fried chicken, place it in a freezer bag and remove all the air you can. When ready to use the chicken, bake it on a buttered baking sheet for 30 minutes at 400 degrees F.

Don't freeze stuffing inside a bird; always pack the stuffing and freeze it separately.

Fish freezes well; just be sure to use a nonporous container. Lean fish will keep for six months and fattier fish will keep for three months.

PASTA

What a time-saver it is to have cooked pasta on hand. It freezes very well, so don't hesitate to keep various kinds in the freezer for salads, soups, and main courses. Just be sure that when you cook it originally, you cook it *al dente*, as it will cook a little more when you reboil it.

MASHED POTATOES

These will keep frozen for one month. Add cream and butter when reheating in a double boiler. My favorite mashed potatoes are whipped up with low-fat cream cheese and minced garlic. (Whole potatoes often turn mushy in the freezer; if you have a favorite recipe that calls for potatoes, try to add the potatoes after the dish is thawed and ready for reheating.)

BREADS AND MUFFINS

Our kids zoom through so many sandwiches that we're always reaching into the freezer to pull out another loaf of bread. To thaw bread, just leave it out, wrapped in its plastic bag, at room temperature for a few hours.

TIP:
Next time you make hamburger patties, knead minced fresh herbs into the ground meat.

TIP:

Sautéed frozen chopped onions are easiest to prepare if you sauté them all on cooking day. Sauté first, then measure. Use the 12-ounce packages of frozen chopped onions available in the frozen foods aisle. Each package contains 3 cups of raw chopped onion, and sautées down to 1 1/2 cups. If you prefer to use fresh onion, you can chop your own and freeze it. Or, you can chop the onion on your cooking day, and figure 1 medium onion equals 1/2 cup chopped, sautéed onion.

Flour stores best in the freezer, because you arrest the bacteria that breaks it down. I also like to keep a mix for muffins on hand in the freezer. Then, when we want fresh, steaming muffins (pumpkin is our favorite), all we need to do is add the wet ingredients and bake them. They come out delicious every time. (*See page 37 for a muffin mix recipe that you can divide into ten portions,* each portion making twelve muffins, *and keep in the freezer.*)

I also use a little of my freezer space for frozen bread dough—what a godsend. Besides making "homemade" bread with it, you can make cinnamon rolls or garlic bread sticks, or roll it out for pizza crust. (Roll in some crushed basil or rosemary—yum!)

VEGETABLES

As with any produce, be sure to wash vegetables thoroughly. You have no guarantee of cleanliness at the market, so rinse everything well.

Before you freeze most vegetables, you need to blanch them. This is easy to do. Just place the vegetables in a wire basket or colander, and immerse them in boiling water for 2 to 3 minutes. Be sure not to use a copper or iron pot.

Remove the produce from the hot water, and immediately submerge it in an ice-and-water-filled sink for the same length of time. This prevents further cooking. Now package and freeze your vegetables. When you're ready to use them, you don't need to plan defrosting time; simply cook as if the vegetables were fresh.

Veggies that work well this way (and most will keep up to six months) are asparagus, beans, broccoli, brussels sprouts, cabbage, carrots, cauliflower, celery, corn on the cob (blanch 8 to 10 minutes), greens, okra, peas (blanch for only 90 seconds), and tomatoes (peeled and used only for cooking).

Some vegetables don't need to be blanched before freezing. Onions and bell peppers can be chopped and frozen while fresh. In fact, many of the recipes in this book call for frozen chopped onions—if you freeze several batches of them, your work will be greatly simplified (they're also available in the freezer section of the supermarket). Beets and mushrooms can be cooked just until tender, then frozen. Potatoes, yams, pumpkin, and squashes all freeze best if you cook them and mash them before freezing.

Vegetables that will be added to a casserole should be slightly undercooked when you freeze them, so they can continue cooking when you bake the casserole.

Puréed veggies are great for adding to soups or feeding to a baby. Force the cooked vegetables through a sieve, cool quickly, then package and freeze. Thaw in the top of a double boiler over simmering water.

Before we go any further, I have to give you a great recipe. It's for a wonderful salad that has only four ingredients. You start with blanched, frozen green beans. Let them thaw just until they're no longer frozen but still cool. Drizzle with Paul Newman's Caesar dressing, and sprinkle with bleu cheese. Serve over a leaf of lettuce. Easy, quick, and nutritious.

FRUIT

Freezers make it possible to savor the luscious sweetness of summer even in the dead of winter. There are just a few guidelines to make sure your fruit freezes successfully.

First, don't use overripe fruit or it will turn mushy. The exception is bananas, which you'll use mashed anyway. You can freeze overripe bananas right in the skins, then peel them and add them to shakes, smoothies, pancake batter, cakes, and breads. Try stirring one into cooked carrots to form a sweet glaze. (Sprinkle in some dark raisins for added color and texture.)

Another convenient way to store frozen bananas is to mash them and press them into ice-cube trays for smaller, pop-out portions.

Juicy, sliced fruits are best sprinkled with sugar before freezing; use about 1 cup of sugar to every 4 cups of fruit. To prevent apple, pear, and peach slices from darkening, dab them first with lemon juice, packaged ascorbic acid crystals, or a crushed vitamin C tablet. Steaming also keeps apples and pears from darkening.

Most berries can be "dry frozen" and then loosely packed. Just spread the berries out on a cookie sheet, put them in the freezer, and when frozen, place the berries in a resealable plastic bag. I've had excellent results with blueberries, strawberries, grapes, raspberries, cranberries, pitted plum halves, and melon balls. Pineapple is equally easy; just slice and freeze.

You want to feel old? My friend Karen Rogers made the comment recently that she hoped Paul Newman would win an Academy Award. Her sixteen-year-old daughter, Whitney, and a classmate were there, and the classmate asked, "Who's Paul Newman?"

Whitney said, "You know—the salad dressing guy."

The friend was astounded. "You mean he makes movies, too?"

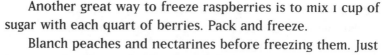

TIP:
Don't refrigerate fruit;
it kills the flavor.
Serve fruit at room
temperature.

Another great way to freeze raspberries is to mix 1 cup of sugar with each quart of berries. Pack and freeze.

Blanch peaches and nectarines before freezing them. Just immerse the fruit in boiling water for 2 minutes. The peels should slip right off. I like to freeze these fruits in a bag along with the sugar, cinnamon, flour, butter (and ascorbic acid powder to prevent darkening) called for in my favorite pie recipe. To serve a fresh peach pie on the spur of the moment, I simply pour the thawed contents of the bag into a crust and bake it. The same would work for a peach cobbler, or for apple pie.

Homemade applesauce is easy to make if you plan ahead just a little. Peel, core, and slice fresh apples. Steam, blanch, or cook them; then if you're freezing them for applesauce, just add sugar and cinnamon. When you're ready for applesauce, simply pour the thawed apple mixture into a saucepan and stir over medium heat.

Other fruits that freeze well in puréed form are apricots, melons, nectarines, peaches, plums, and strawberries. And, of course, all fruit juices freeze well. A great way to entice kids to eat more fruit is to make frozen pops using fruit juice.

DESSERTS

Some of the yummiest desserts keep terrifically in the freezer. Cheesecakes and fruit pies are both good examples. Cakes freeze well, too. In fact, a professional baker taught me to freeze any cake before you frost it, so it won't tear and get crumbs in the frosting.

Pie pastry can also be frozen. Just flatten it out inside a resealable bag, then stack the crusts like pizzas. I highly recommend making your own piecrust for several reasons. First, it's far more economical. But even more important, it's simply better looking and better tasting. Homemade pie dough can be rolled out thicker and turns out flakier than store-bought. *(See pages 24–25 for two of my piecrust recipes.)*

Store fruit, berry, pumpkin, and chiffon pies, cooked or uncooked, in a waxed box. To keep the crusts from getting soggy, coat the bottom crust with melted butter before filling. I don't recommend freezing cream or custard pies; they tend to separate when frozen.

Cookie dough, my all-time favorite splurge food, freezes wonderfully. If you're a mom who feels guilty about not bringing homemade cookies to school and scout functions, here's a way that you can amaze and impress everyone. One evening or Saturday morning, make a quadruple batch of cookie dough. *(See page 122 for a recipe for basic cookie dough.)* Freeze it in little balls on cookie sheets (otherwise you have to thaw the entire batch of dough before you can work with it). When the dough balls have frozen, dump them into a freezer bag or a plastic container. Then, when you're ready for fresh-baked cookies, all you need to do is take out the number of dough balls you need, set them on a cookie sheet, and bake. There's no prep time and, if you use baking parchment, no cleanup. Now *that's* a double treat.

Or, bake the cookies when you have time, and freeze them. Well-wrapped cookies will keep in the freezer up to six months.

TIP:
Freeze softened ice cream in a piecrust for a fast dessert.

Freezing Meal Components

In addition to freezing individual foods, you can freeze many of the prepared components that go into entire meals. Then, when making a recipe, much of your footwork is already done. Here are some staples to keep on hand in the freezer, as space allows:

Cooked stuffing
Ground beef cooked with frozen chopped onions
Grated cheese (don't thaw when you need to use it; grated
    cheese warms quickly and can go right from freezer to recipe)
Cooked rice
Spaghetti sauce
Stock *(See pages 23–24 for instructions on making stock.)*
Stews
Cooked chicken—both whole pieces and diced
Ham slices
Tortillas
Bread crumbs (for crab or salmon cakes, meat loaf, breading fish
    or chicken, or topping a casserole; whirl already seasoned
    breadsticks or bread in food processor or blender)
Herbs (blanch in boiling water for 10 minutes, pat dry, freeze in
    small resealable bags)
Flour, powdered gluten, dry milk—wrapped tightly
Nuts
Cubes of white sauce mix *(See recipe on page 24.)*

TIP:

When cooking in the microwave, figure meals will take one-fourth of the cooking time than in a standard oven.

I wouldn't freeze a mayonnaise-based recipe, but sandwiches made with mayonnaise freeze just fine.

Freezing Meals

You can freeze entire meals in a stack. Portion out the parts of each meal on a divided foil tray. Or you can wrap each part of the meal in foil or place in a foil cooking pouch, place all the parts on a stiff paper plate, and wrap everything again in foil. Or, if you plan to use a microwave oven, wrap them in paper or plastic instead. To keep meats moist, cover them with gravy or a sauce. To keep vegetables moist, use a sauce or butter.

Label the trays "Monday," "Tuesday," and so on. If you prefer to package the meal components separately, just label and stack all the Monday parts together, all the Tuesday parts together, and so on. This is a slam dunk!

When you're ready to make dinner, bake the prepared meals at 375 degrees F for 40 minutes. Or, if you're using a microwave, cook for 10 minutes at full power for every 2 cups of frozen food (consult your oven manual for exact times). Remember to stir a couple of times during baking and before serving.

Freezing Don'ts

Some foods simply don't freeze well. They separate, wilt, turn grainy, or crumble. Don't freeze:

Mayonnaise	Cucumbers
Eggs in the shell	Celery
Hard-cooked egg whites	Gelatin
Boiled potatoes	Meringue
Lettuce and other greens	Custards
Radishes	Boiled frostings

variations on a theme: the basics

One way to cook a week's worth of meals efficiently is to use basic stocks, sauces, baking dough, and mixes that can be prepared in advance and each day transformed into a meal. You can take a basic ground beef mix and make it into a meat loaf, a pizza, a casserole, a soup—and so on. Stocks and sauces can serve as the base for dozens of recipes, and homemade frozen piecrusts can be used to make quiches, pot pies, and desserts in (almost) a flash.

Stock

Using this magic ingredient that can be prepared in advance, you can make fabulous-tasting soups, gravies, and marinades, almost without lifting a finger.

Stock is not some hard-to-find product that's used only by professional chefs; it's the "secret ingredient" used by most home-style cooks as well. When you cook rice, vegetables, meats—anything savory, really—you should use liquid that has some flavor to it, not just tap water. This flavored liquid is called "stock," and you make it by saving the liquid left over from cooking vegetables and meat.

To make vegetable stock, grind up cooked veggies (Try a mixture of onions, carrots, and celery, which the French call *mire poix*) in your blender, then add equal parts water. Don't forget your favorite herbs (but remember that herbs intensify when frozen, so watch that garlic). When you've blended your vegetables and water, strain the mixture to remove large particles, and freeze it (for three months maximum).

23

TIP:

To remove fat from
soup, drop in a few
lettuce leaves. The
fat will cling to the
leaves, then you can
discard them.

You can make chicken stock by boiling chicken (or chicken parts like backs, necks, and gizzards) and saving the leftover water. Strain the stock, then chill it so the fat will rise and solidify and you can remove it. If you cook the liquid down a bit, you'll have a tasty, concentrated stock to freeze.

Meat stock can be made from the juices of cooked meat, and also by simmering beef or veal bones. As with chicken stock, chill the stock, remove the fat, then freeze it in usable quantities.

I like to freeze stock in ice-cube trays, so I can take out small amounts without thawing a huge brick of it. To free up your ice-cube trays, you can store the frozen cubes loosely in a freezer bag. A convenient alternative is canned stock or broth. Though it doesn't quite taste the same as homemade, it does make life simpler.

Piecrusts

Here's my favorite piecrust recipe. Yes, it contains lard; yes, it's the best piecrust you've ever eaten—hey, if you're worried about fat, you shouldn't be eating pie in the first place.

Flaky Pie Pastry

Makes 2 piecrusts

1	cup all-purpose flour
1	cup cake flour
1/2	teaspoon salt
1/2	cup lard, cut into pieces
4	tablespoons butter (1/2 stick)
7	tablespoons ice water

Work with chilled ingredients. Combine flours and salt in a large bowl. Cut in lard and butter with two knives, or with pastry blender, until flour forms coarse crumbs. Stir in water until dough forms a ball. Knead briefly on a floured surface until smooth. Divide in half. Chill, covered, for 30 minutes or more.

For those of you who will gladly eat solid shortening but cringe at the thought of lard, here's another tried-and-true winner.

Easy Pie Dough

Makes 2 pie crusts

2	cups all-purpose flour
1	teaspoon salt
2/3	cup solid shortening
	Ice water to moisten

Cut flour and salt into shortening until mixture forms coarse crumbs. Add ice water until dough forms a soft ball. Roll out on floured surface.

Mixes

Basic mixes make spur-of-the-moment cooking easy. Mixes won't give you the dazzle and variety of the recipes that I've included in the later chapters of this book, but if it's simplicity you're after, mixes will do the trick. Following are three basic mixes that you can freeze, and dozens of easy ways to use them.

These mixes can find their way into your favorite soup and casserole recipes, too. Be adventurous—stir them into scrambled eggs, add them to canned soups—the possibilities are endless.

White Sauce Mix

2	tablespoons butter (may vary)
2	tablespoons flour (may vary)
1	cup milk
	Salt and pepper to taste

Mix equal parts butter and flour, stirring into a paste. Freeze in 1-tablespoon balls, or in the cubes of an ice-cube tray.

To make a quick white sauce, simmer 2 tablespoon-cubes of the frozen butter and flour mixture with milk, then salt and pepper to taste.

TIP:

Knead 1/4 cup of finely crushed nuts into your next piecrust for a flavorful variation.

Beef Mix

3	pounds ground beef (or lamb or pork)
1	cup frozen chopped onion
1	cup chopped bell pepper
1	can (16 ounces) tomatoes
1	can (8 ounces) tomato paste
	Garlic to taste

Simmer all ingredients until meat is cooked and onion is transparent. Divide mixture into three freezing containers. One portion can be used in any of the following recipes, which each serve 4 to 6 (unless otherwise specified).

Beef Barley Soup

1	container frozen beef mix, thawed
2	cans (15 ounces) beef broth (or 4 cups homemade beef stock)
2	cups cooked barley
2	cups diced vegetables of your choice (mixed work well)

Combine beef mix with other ingredients and heat in a saucepan over moderate heat.

Texas Chili

1	container frozen beef mix, thawed
1	can (15 ounces) kidney beans
1	tablespoon chili powder
1	can (15 ounces) beef broth (or 2 cups homemade beef stock)
	Hot sauce to taste

Combine beef mix with kidney beans, chili powder, and beef broth or stock; heat in saucepan over moderate heat. Season with hot sauce to taste.

Some of my recipes specify canned tomatoes and other canned ingredients. This is for simplicity's sake. If you prefer to stew your own tomatoes, by all means do that instead.

Spaghetti

1	container frozen beef mix, thawed
1	can or bottle (15 ounces) spaghetti sauce
1	package (1 pound) spaghetti noodles, cooked and drained

Combine beef mix and spaghetti sauce in saucepan over moderate heat to desired temperature. Serve over spaghetti noodles.

Lasagna

Makes 8 to 10 servings

1	container frozen beef mix, thawed
1	can (15 ounces) tomato sauce
	Oregano and basil to taste
1	package (8 ounces) lasagna noodles, cooked and drained
3/4	pound mozzarella cheese, sliced or grated
1	carton (8 ounces) ricotta cheese
1/2	cup grated Parmesan cheese

Preheat oven to 350 degrees F. Combine beef mix with tomato sauce, oregano, and basil, then layer cooked lasagna noodles, beef mixture, and cheeses three times in a 9 × 13-inch baking dish. Bake for 15 minutes.

VARIATION: Use sliced flour tortillas in place of lasagna noodles.

Tacos

Makes 8 tacos

1	container frozen beef mix, thawed
1	envelope taco seasoning mix
8	corn or flour tortillas (10 inches each)
2	cups shredded fresh lettuce
2 1/2	cups grated Cheddar cheese
1	tomato, chopped

Combine beef mix and taco seasoning mix; heat in saucepan over moderate heat. Serve in warm tortillas with lettuce, cheese, and tomato.

Quickie Stroganoff

1	container frozen beef mix, thawed
1	can (15 ounces) beef broth (or 2 cups homemade beef broth or stock)
1	can (3 ounces) sliced mushrooms
1	teaspoon Worcestershire sauce
1	cup sour cream
1	pound (or about 6 cups) cooked noodles or rice

Combine beef mix with beef broth or stock, mushrooms, Worcestershire sauce, and sour cream. Simmer until heated through and sauce thickens, about 10 minutes. Serve over noodles or rice.

Old-Fashioned Pizza

1	store-bought, baked pizza crust (12 inches)
1	cup store-bought pizza sauce
1	container frozen beef mix, thawed
2	cups grated mozzarella cheese

Preheat oven to 425 degrees F. Cover pizza crust with pizza sauce, beef mix, and cheese. Bake about 15 minutes, until cheese is bubbly.

Taco Casserole

Makes 6 to 8 servings

1	envelope taco seasoning mix
1	container frozen beef mix, thawed
1	dozen corn tortillas, sliced into 2-inch-wide strips
1	can (15 ounces) enchilada sauce
3	cups grated Cheddar cheese

Preheat oven to 350 degrees F. In a medium-size bowl, add taco seasoning mix to beef mix. In a 9 × 13-inch baking dish, layer the beef and seasoning mix with tortillas, enchilada sauce, and cheese. Repeat layers three times, ending with cheese. Bake for 25 minutes.

Pinwheel Beefwiches

1	container frozen beef mix, thawed
1	package (8 ounces) herb-seasoned cream cheese
4 to 6	flour tortillas (10 inches each)

Heat thawed beef mix in a large skillet over medium-low heat, stirring until thoroughly heated (about 5 minutes). Spread cream cheese over flour tortillas, sprinkle with the warm beef mix, and roll up tightly. Eat burrito-style.

VARIATION: Try flavored tortillas.

Thai Beef and Pasta

1	container frozen beef mix, thawed and heated
1	package (1 pound) angel hair pasta, cooked and drained
1	cup snow peas
1/2	cup peanuts
1	tablespoon Thai seasoning spice

Mix beef mix, pasta, snow peas, peanuts, and seasoning spice in a large skillet over medium-low heat. Serve hot.

Poultry Mix (Chicken or Turkey)

3	pounds boneless poultry
2	cups milk
1	cup frozen chopped onion, thawed
4	tablespoon-cubes frozen white sauce mix *(see page 24)*
6	ounces cream cheese, softened
1	teaspoon minced garlic
	Salt and pepper to taste
1	can (6 ounces) mushrooms (optional)

Simmer poultry meat in a large stockpot of water until cooked. (Reserve water for soup stock, if desired). Or, microwave on high for 10 to 15 minutes, checking frequently and removing poultry from microwave when juices run clear. Cool and chop. Mix poultry with remaining ingredients in same pot, stirring over medium-low heat until cheese melts and sauce thickens. Let the poultry mix cool, then divide into three portions and freeze. One portion can be used in each of the following recipes (which searve 4–6 unless otherwise specified).

Chicken or Turkey Pot Pie

1	cup diced potatoes
1	cup diced vegetables (peas and carrots are good)
1	container frozen poultry mix, thawed
1	pre-made, unbaked piecrust (9 inches), thawed

Preheat oven to 450 degrees F. Add potatoes and vegetables to poultry mix in a large bowl. Pour into 1 1/2-quart casserole dish and top with piecrust, crimping edges to seal. Vent with fork. Bake for 25 minutes.

Chicken–Red Pepper Casserole

1	container frozen poultry mix, thawed
1/2	cup store-bought buttermilk baking mix
3	eggs
1	cup grated cheese (any kind)
1	cup store-bought roasted red peppers, chopped

Preheat oven to 400 degrees F. Butter a 10-inch baking dish. In a large bowl, combine poultry mix, baking mix, eggs, cheese, and red peppers. Mix thoroughly and pour into buttered baking dish. Bake for 25 minutes.

Pasta Primavera

1	container frozen poultry mix, thawed
2	cups frozen chopped vegetables*
1/4	cup whole-grain mustard (optional)
1	package (1 pound) pasta (any type), cooked and drained

Combine poultry mix and vegetables; heat in saucepan over low heat. If you like, add whole-grain mustard. Toss with your favorite cooked pasta.

*Some tasty vegetable suggestions: asparagus tips, carrots, and yellow squash.

TIP:

Keep your hands clean when you butter a baking dish by slipping a plastic bag over your hand, then dipping into the butter and rubbing it on the baking dish with the plastic bag.

Cream of Corn and Chicken Soup

1	container frozen poultry mix, thawed
1	package (16 ounces) frozen corn
1	can (15 ounces) creamed corn
1	cup diced potato
3	cans (15 ounces each) chicken broth (or 6 cups homemade chicken broth or stock)
	Dash of Tabasco sauce

In a large soup pot, combine poultry mix with corn, potato, and chicken broth or stock. Give it some zing with a dash of Tabasco. Heat to desired temperature over medium heat. Do not boil.

Creamy Chinese Casserole

1	container frozen poultry mix, thawed
1	ramen soup and seasoning package
2	cups grated cabbage
1	can (8 ounces) sliced water chestnuts
1	package (10 ounces) frozen snow peas, thawed
1	pound (about 6 cups) rice, cooked

Preheat oven to 350 degrees F. Stir together poultry mix with crumbled ramen noodles and ramen seasoning packet, cabbage, water chestnuts, and snow peas. Bake in 9 × 13-inch baking dish for 25 minutes. Serve over hot rice.

Turkey or Chicken Melts

1	container frozen poultry mix, thawed
6	sandwich buns
1 to 2	tomatoes, sliced
	Jack cheese slices

Pile thawed poultry mix onto sandwich buns, top with slices of tomato and cheese. Broil until cheese is bubbly, 2 to 3 minutes.

VARIATION: Add a slice of ham, and substitute Swiss cheese for Jack to make Cordon Bleu Melts.

Broccoli Casserole

1	teaspoon curry powder
1	container frozen poultry mix, thawed
3	cups fresh or frozen broccoli
2	cups grated Cheddar cheese
1/2	cup bread crumbs

Preheat oven to 350 degrees F. Mix curry powder into poultry mix. Arrange broccoli in a 9 × 13-inch baking dish, then pour mix over broccoli. Top with cheese and bread crumbs. Bake for 25 minutes.

Mideast "Cobb" Salad

1	container frozen poultry mix, thawed
1	cucumber, chopped
1	tomato, chopped
1	bunch fresh spinach, chopped
	Dash of lemon juice
1 to 2	tablespoons hummus
	Crumbled feta cheese (optional)
	Oregano (optional)
	Olives (optional)

In a large bowl, mix thawed poultry mix with cucumber, tomato, and spinach. Stir in lemon juice and hummus. Go Greek by adding crumbled feta cheese, oregano, and juicy olives. Serve cold.

Chicken Vegetable Pizza

1	container frozen poultry mix, thawed
1	store-bought, baked pizza crust (12 inches)
2	cups thawed, frozen vegetables of your choice
2	cups grated mozzarella cheese

Heat broiler. Spread poultry mix on pizza crust. Sprinkle with vegetables, and top with cheese. Broil until cheese is bubbly, 2 to 3 minutes.

Provence Salad

1	container frozen poultry mix, thawed
1	can (2 ounces) anchovies
1	clove garlic, crushed
1/2	cup green beans
1/2	cup chopped zucchini
1/2	cup chopped roasted red peppers
1/2	cup chopped eggplant
1/2	cup chopped tomatoes
1	scoop olive tapenade (optional)
1	tablespoon capers (optional)
	Zucchini blossoms (optional, for garnish)

Bottled crushed garlic is easy to use—but remember, there's no way to beat the flavor of fresh garlic!

In a large bowl, combine poultry mix with anchovies, garlic, green beans, zucchini, red peppers, eggplant, and tomatoes. For extra pizzazz, stir in olive tapenade and capers. Garnish with zucchini blossoms, if desired.

Polynesian Bake

1	container frozen poultry mix, thawed
1/2	cup mango chutney
1	can (15 ounces) crushed pineapple, drained
3	cups cooked rice
1	tablespoon Jerk seasoning

Preheat oven to 350 degrees F. Mix poultry mix with chutney, pineapple, rice, and Jerk seasoning. Bake in 9 × 13-inch dish for 15 minutes.

Seafood Mix

3	pounds seafood (shellfish, fish filets, crab, shrimp, salmon, snapper, white fish, cod, or any of your other favorites), cut into bite-sized pieces
1	can (15 ounces) tomato sauce
1	can (8 ounces) tomato paste

Simmer all ingredients just until fish is cooked. Freeze in three equal portions. Each portion may be thawed and used to make the following recipes (which serve 4–6 unless otherwise specified).

Variations on a Theme: The Basics

Seafood Wraps

Makes 8 servings

1	container frozen seafood mix, thawed
1	cup fresh chopped vegetables of your choice*
3	tablespoon-cubes frozen white sauce
2	cups grated Cheddar cheese
8	flour tortillas (10-inches each)

Combine seafood mix with vegetables and white sauce in a large saucepan over medium-low heat. Stir in cheese just until it melts. Spoon mixture into flour tortillas and wrap.

Seafood Ratatouille

1	container frozen seafood mix, thawed
4	cups chopped fresh vegetables†
3	cups cooked rice

Combine seafood mix with vegetables; heat in saucepan over moderate heat, stirring for 5 minutes. Serve over hot rice.

Barbecued Seafood Pizza

1	container frozen seafood mix, thawed
1	cup barbecue sauce
1	store-bought, baked pizza crust (12 inches)
1/2	red onion, chopped
2	cups grated mozzarella cheese

Heat broiler. Combine seafood mix with barbecue sauce and spread over pizza crust. Top with red onion and cheese. Broil until cheese is bubbly, 2 to 3 minutes.

*Some tasty vegetable suggestions: asparagus, cabbage, mushrooms, zucchini, onions, and peppers.

†Some tasty vegetable suggestions: eggplant, zucchini, squash, onions, beans, and peppers.

The Once-a-Week Cookbook

Fish Tacos

Makes 8 tacos

1	container frozen seafood mix, thawed
1	envelope taco seasoning
8	tortillas
1/2	cup sour cream
2	cups grated Cheddar cheese
2	cups fresh shredded lettuce
1 to 2	tomatoes, chopped

Combine seafood mix with taco seasoning; heat in a medium saucepan over moderate heat for 5 minutes. Spoon mixture into tortillas, and top with sour cream, cheese, lettuce, and tomatoes.

Seafood Quiche

1	container frozen seafood mix, thawed
2	cups milk
1	cup store-bought buttermilk baking mix
4	eggs
2	cups grated Jack cheese

Preheat oven to 400 degrees F. Butter 10-inch baking dish. In a large bowl, mix seafood mix thoroughly with milk, baking mix, eggs, and cheese. Pour into buttered baking dish. Bake for 40 minutes.

Seafood and Pasta

1	container frozen seafood mix, thawed
1	package (1 pound) pasta (any type), cooked and drained Salt and black pepper

Mix seafood mix with your favorite cooked pasta. Add salt and black pepper to taste. Serve hot or cold.

Seafood Salad

1	container frozen seafood mix, thawed
1	cup frozen peas, thawed
1	cup chopped cucumber
4	hard-boiled eggs, sliced
2	cups cooked small-shell macaroni, drained
	Horseradish to taste

Toss seafood mix with peas, cucumber, egg slices, and macaroni. Add horseradish to taste.

Mediterranean Couscous

1	container frozen seafood mix, thawed
4	cups cooked couscous
1	cup sliced olives (black, green, or Mediterranean)
1	cup crumbled feta cheese
	Spritz of olive oil
	Juice of 1 lemon
	Mint leaves

Stir seafood mix with couscous, olives, feta cheese, olive oil, and lemon juice in a large bowl. Garnish with mint leaves and serve hot or cold.

Seafood Tuscany

1	container frozen seafood mix, thawed
1	package (25 ounces) cheese tortellini, cooked and drained
1	cup store-bought pesto sauce
1	cup sliced olives
1/2	cup chopped onion
	Handful of fresh basil
1/2	cup grated fresh Parmesan cheese

Heat seafood mix in saucepan over medium heat. Toss with cooked tortellini, pesto sauce, olives, onion, basil, and cheese.

TIP:

Put olive or cooking oil into spray bottles and you'll use less.

Muffin Mix

The following mix is simple, tasty, and can be used as the basis for any number of delicious muffin recipes. Freeze it and keep it on hand.

Easy Muffins

5	pounds plus 4 cups all-purpose flour
9 1/3	cups sugar
9 1/3	cups dry milk
2/3	cup baking powder
3	tablespoons plus 1 teaspoon salt
1	egg
3/4	cup water
1/2	cup oil
1/2	cup fruit (diced apples, raspberries, blueberries, raisins, nuts, bananas, or pumpkin)

Mix the dry ingredients in a very large bowl or roasting pan, then divide mixture among 10 resealable freezer bags. Each mix will yield 12 muffins.

When ready to bake, no thawing is necessary. Simply stir one bag's contents in a large bowl with the egg, water, oil, and fruit.

Preheat oven to 350 degrees F. Grease bottoms of 12 muffin cups. Divide batter among cups. Bake for 20 minutes, or until muffins are golden.

kids in the kitchen

Years ago my friend Cynthia Rhine made one simple comment that changed everything about my attitude toward my children. "If you can read, you can do laundry," she said, explaining why her young son, Aaron, was so adept at household chores.

From that moment on, I saw my kids as adults in the making—people who could learn far more than I'd given them credit for. Large families—families with ten and eleven kids—have this figured out. The minute a kid is old enough, he's diapering babies, making beds and sandwiches, and providing help that is desperately needed while Mom is bathing or nursing another child.

This is how kids grew up a few generations ago, when more people farmed and counted on their kids as extra workers. Little kids lugged buckets of milk that weighed almost as much as they did. They kneaded bread and plucked chickens—they grew up *skilled.*

Today's kids are soft. (My eldest just filled out a camp form and wrote "manual labor" under "allergies.") They're used to an automated, computerized, throwaway world, where convenience is king. They know how to program a computer, but not how to pre-soak a pair of socks.

So I decided to change all that. Our kids have to do their own laundry; pitch in with yard work; scrub toilets; wash windows; and, yep, help with the cooking.

Don't wait until kids are teenagers to teach them how to scramble an egg. By then they've seen thousands of meals magically appear on their plates, and they might be content to let the magician keep his tricks to himself.

"Happy is the family which can eat onions together. They are, for the time being, separate from the world and have a harmony of aspiration."

—Charles Dudley Warner

Start when a child is three years old. Let her put the napkins out. Let him bring in the spoons. Let her pour ingredients into a bowl. He can drizzle honey onto a slice of toast. She can shake chicken in a resealable bag, to coat it with crumbs. He can roll cookie balls, or pat a meat loaf into shape.

Don't be a parent who calls, "Dinner's ready." Be a parent who calls, "Time to make dinner," and expects full participation. Not only does it make preparation easier and quicker (eventually), but you'll give your kids an important ingredient of self-esteem: competence. When kids have skills, they feel capable, smart, and needed. And they are!

The kids will have smoother transitions into adulthood, too. And they'll thank you for teaching them the life skills they don't learn in school. No matter how much you emphasize academics or the extracurricular activities we give kids today, be sure you teach your children how to survive on their own.

A bonus to all this training is that your child becomes a leader. She's the one at school who knows how to clean up in chemistry class. He's the one whose girlfriends think it's cool that he irons his own shirts and makes homemade donuts. She's the one whose boss gives her a great letter of recommendation into an Ivy League school, because her boss saw what a self-starter that young woman is. And what do those kids think? They're proud of themselves, that's what.

The freezer techniques in this book are intended to give you more time with your friends or family. And they do. But preparing and cooking meals together can also be fun family time. Don't look at these blocks of cooking time as lonely hours in the kitchen. Delegate. Give everybody an assignment. A ten-year-old can sauté the chopped onions. A teenager can use a knife to cut up vegetables. Somebody can be in charge of timing the baked items. Someone else can do all the cleanup. Trade jobs the next week, so nobody gets bored and everyone gets good training. I have one friend whose kids know that Saturday morning is chore time (or it could be family cooking time), and after that, the day is theirs. It's become such a tradition that no one questions it; they all simply get up and pitch in.

You will honestly wonder why you ever did it any other way.

The Once-a-Week Cookbook

Lunches

Kids should absolutely prepare their own lunches. Supervise to make sure they're not just taking candy and chips to school, but let them be the ones to stockpile five lunches in the freezer (we do this on Sunday night). This way, every day they simply pull one out, maybe add a piece of fresh fruit or some juice, and away they go. You can still add napkins with notes or stickers on them, or an occasional surprise treat.

When kids make their sandwiches, let them use flavored butters and cream cheeses for spreads. You can make your own flavored butters and cheeses by softening 4 ounces of butter or cream cheese, and mashing in a teaspoon of any of the following:

Italian herbs (fresh or dried)	Chili powder
Tarragon	Minced carrot
Fennel	Minced onion
Basil	Minced bell pepper
Oregano	Minced chilies
Thyme	Lemon pepper
Chopped cilantro	Worcestershire sauce
Pickle relish	Minced dried fruit
Chopped olives	Minced apple
Crushed garlic	Crushed pineapple
Minced celery	Coconut
Chopped pimiento	Coarse ground pepper
Crushed capers	Celery seed
Ethnic spice blends	Bacon bits
Cinnamon	Sesame seeds
	Shelled sunflower seeds

A frozen sandwich will keep other foods in the lunch box or backpack cold and will defrost in time for lunch. Kids can add fresh lettuce and tomatoes to their lunch boxes before they leave the house in the morning, then assemble the sandwich when they sit down to eat.

Many of the recipes in this book can be used for lunches as well as for dinners. Simply freeze the food in one-serving containers that will thaw by lunchtime. And don't forget that cheeses, dried fruits, nuts, pickles, olives, cherries, and many fresh fruits are terrific to freeze just as they are *(see chapter 3)*.

Think of leftovers as sandwich ingredients. Many of the recipes in this book can be piled onto a 6-inch sandwich bun, covered with cheese, and broiled for a delicious melt.

Here are fifteen more easy concoctions to freeze for lunches:

- Mix 1/2 cup each of drained canned fruit cocktail, sour cream, and thawed whipped topping, and freeze in small lidded plastic containers. Be sure to pack plastic spoons.

- Roll up flour tortillas spread with a flavored cream cheese, a few slices of lunch meat, and some grated Cheddar. Slice into 1-inch-wide pinwheels and freeze in plastic containers. Then pack as many pinwheels as you'd like in plastic wrap.

- Freeze individual cake slices in plastic bags or containers, and freeze frosting in separate, small resealable plastic bags. Your child can take a slice of cake and one small bag of frosting, and frost the cake during lunch. (Snip a corner of the bag and squeeze the frosting out. Hands stay clean, too!)

- Make a few dozen cracker-cheese-lunch meat "sandwiches," and freeze four or five in one plastic bag. It takes a lot less time when you create an assembly line and make them in bulk.

- Spread pizza sauce on a bagel; top with a slab of mozzarella. Melt in the microwave, then freeze.

- Freeze cold pasta salad in individual serving–sized plastic containers. My kids like cooked corkscrew pasta mixed with chunks of ham and Thousand Island dressing. It couldn't be easier.

- Chopped black olives, onions, and Cheddar cheese are a great flavor combination. Mix some together, moisten with a little butter or cream cheese, and spread it onto buns or bread slices.

- Spread a deli-thin slice of ham with cream cheese. Wrap it around a whole dill pickle. Slice and freeze, or freeze it whole. This is another great flavor combo.

- Toss tuna, chopped onion, and a squeeze of lemon together. Freeze in a plastic bag. Send it to school with a purchased package of mayonnaise like condiment stands offer. At school, your youngster can squeeze the mayonnaise into the plastic bag, mix everything together, and have a tuna spread for a roll or a pita pocket.

The Once-a-Week Cookbook

- Freeze a few slices of pizza whenever you have it for dinner. Wrap in foil and send a slice to school.

- Mix 2 tablespoons of granola into a small carton of yogurt and freeze. By lunchtime, it will be ready to eat with a spoon.

- Wrap a slice of cheese and a slice of ham around a breadstick and freeze it, packing tightly so it won't uncurl.

- Mix cooked shrimp and cooked pasta with shrimp cocktail sauce. Freeze in one-portion containers. Pack a plastic fork.

- Load an ice cream cone with pudding and freeze. Cover the open end with plastic wrap. By lunchtime, it'll be just right to enjoy with a spoon.

- Frozen crab or salmon cakes make yummy lunches. Just send them along with a frozen sandwich bun and a little packet of mustard.

breakfasts on the go

The cook-ahead-and-freeze-it method works for breakfasts, too. Think of your most hectic time of day: the morning, when everybody's rushing off to work and school, right? Every second counts as we dash from shower to shuttle, and most of us end up going the cold cereal route. After all, who has time for a scrumptious hot breakfast?

You do. With everything already prepared and waiting, it takes less time to warm up one of these yummy creations than to make toast and cereal. Breakfast really can be more of a meal, and less of a grab-and-run.

Here are some perfect foods to freeze for quick preparation in the mornings.

TIP:
Fry bacon with maple syrup and cracked pepper for a new twist on a breakfast favorite.

Waffles

Wait—before you say, "Waffles—are you kidding?" remember that these are made ahead of time, divided into four sections, and frozen. You just pop them into the toaster and you're off to heaven.

Apple Oatmeal Waffles

1 1/2	cups all-purpose flour
1	cup oats
1	tablespoon baking powder
1/2	teaspoon cinnamon
1/2	teaspoon cloves
1/2	teaspoon nutmeg
1/4	teaspoon salt

TIP:
Keep some
powdered sugar
in a lidded shaker
for dusting cakes,
orange sections,
waffles, and
French toast.

2	eggs
1 1/2	cups buttermilk
4	tablespoons melted butter
2	tablespoons brown sugar
1	small apple, peeled and chopped
1/2	cup chopped nuts (optional)

In a large bowl, mix the flour, oats, baking powder, cinnamon, cloves, nutmeg, and salt. In a small bowl, mix the eggs, buttermilk, butter, and brown sugar. Combine the wet mixture with the dry mixture. Add the apple and nuts. Pour into a waffle iron and bake according to appliance instructions. Freeze.

Pumpkin Waffles

2	cups all-purpose flour
2	teaspoons baking powder
1/4	teaspoon cinnamon
1/4	teaspoon ginger
1/4	teaspoon nutmeg
1/2	teaspoon salt
3	eggs, beaten
1 3/4	cups milk
3/4	cup solid pack pumpkin
1/2	cup vegetable oil

Mix flour, baking powder, cinnamon, ginger, nutmeg, and salt in a large bowl. In a small bowl, mix eggs, milk, pumpkin, and oil. Combine both mixtures, and bake in waffle iron according to appliance instructions. Freeze.

Biscuits

If you keep a bag of biscuit mix in the freezer, you can whip up homemade biscuits just by adding the ingredients that create variations. Or, make them up ahead of time and freeze them already baked. Then, make a quick breakfast sandwich by slipping in a cooked sausage patty or some scrambled eggs.

Easiest Biscuits

2	cups store-bought buttermilk baking mix
3/4	cup milk

Preheat oven to 450 degrees F. Combine ingredients to form dough, then drop by spoonfuls onto an ungreased baking sheet (or roll out the dough and cut circles). Bake for 8 to 10 minutes, or until golden.

Homemade Basic Biscuit Mix

If you'd rather make your own biscuit mix, here's how.

2	cups all-purpose flour
4	teaspoons baking powder
1	tablespoon sugar
1/2	teaspoon baking soda
1/2	teaspoon salt
1/4	cup shortening
3/4	cup buttermilk

Combine dry ingredients in a large bowl, then cut in shortening with two knives until mixture forms coarse crumbs. Freeze.

When ready to bake, preheat oven to 450 degrees F. Add buttermilk to biscuit mix. Drop by spoonfuls onto ungreased baking sheet, or roll out and cut circles. Bake for 8 to 10 minutes, or until golden.

VARIATIONS: When you get to the point where you add the buttermilk, try these variations also:

1. Raisin Cinnamon: Add 1/2 cup raisins and 2 teaspoons cinnamon.

2. Garlic Cheese: Add 1/2 cup grated Cheddar cheese and 1/4 teaspoon garlic powder.

3. Jamaican: Add 1 teaspoon Caribbean Jerk Seasoning spice and 1/2 cup crushed pineapple, drained and squeezed dry.

4. Italian: Add 1/2 cup sun-dried tomatoes, drained and chopped, and 1/2 teaspoon each basil, oregano, and crushed garlic.

5. Mexican: Add 1/4 cup chopped mild green chilies, 1 cup finely grated Cheddar cheese, and 1/2 cup corn.

6. Banana Nut: Add 1/2 cup mashed ripe banana and 1/2 cup chopped nuts.

7. Sweet Potato: Decrease milk to 1/3 cup. Add 3/4 cup puréed sweet potatoes, 2 tablespoons maple syrup, and 1/2 teaspoon each of cinnamon and ginger.

8. Cran-Orange: Add 1/2 cup cranberries and 1 teaspoon orange zest.

9. Blueberry: Add 1/2 cup blueberries.

10. Lemon Poppy Seed: Add 1 teaspoon lemon zest and 1 tablespoon poppy seeds.

TIP:

Before adding berries to bread, cake, or biscuit batter, coat the berries with flour to prevent sinking.

Mini Munchies

These can be topped a zillion different ways to make a nutritious, quick breakfast. Keep the muffins and the toppers frozen, then put them together in the morning.

English Muffins and Bagels

1. Sassy: Spread with cream cheese, top with a scoop of salsa, then add a pinch of grated Cheddar. Microwave or broil just until heated through.

2. Caribbean: Top with Cool Pineapple Salsa (page 87) or Jamaican Salsa (page 180) and a dab of sour cream. You can zap it in the microwave for one minute also, if you want it hot.

3. Red Pepper: Cover with slices of bottled roasted red pepper, then a slab of Monterey Jack cheese. Microwave or broil until cheese melts.

4. Mushroom: Top with sliced mushrooms, drizzle with Italian dressing, then microwave or broil until heated through.

5. Tuna or Crab: Mix tuna or crab with cream cheese and 1/2 teaspoon onion powder. Spread onto muffin and microwave or broil.

6. Cheddar: Mix 1/2 cup soft cream cheese, 1/2 cup grated Cheddar, 2 tablespoons chopped black olives, and 1/2 teaspoon onion powder. Spread on muffins and freeze. When you're ready to enjoy them, microwave or grill until bubbly.

7. Ham: Slather with deviled ham spread and top with a round slice of pineapple.

8. Strawberry: Spread with soft cream cheese, sprinkle with brown sugar, and top with strawberry slices.

9. Peppers: When you're sautéing bell peppers, freeze some for a breakfast topper—simply mix with scrambled eggs and place on a muffin or bagel.

10. Sweet: Mix 1/3 cup cream cheese with 1 tablespoon of powdered sugar. Spread on muffin or bagel, then top with fruit, like a fruit pizza.

11. Dessert: Top a muffin or bagel with ice cream, nuts, and chocolate fudge sauce.

12. Blueberry: Mix 1 teaspoon of lemon zest with 1/2 cup soft cream cheese. Spread onto muffins, then sprinkle with granola and blueberries.

13. Italian: Top a bagel with a slab of mozzarella, a slice of tomato, and a drizzle of Italian dressing. Microwave or broil until cheese melts.

A Traditional Favorite

There are endless variations of this easy recipe. Following are two of my favorites. Use 2 cans of store-bought refrigerator biscuits, separated. Dip them into the following easy blends, then bake in a Bundt pan at 400 degrees F for 10 to 15 minutes:

Monkey Bread

1. Orange: In a medium saucepan over medium-low heat, melt 1/2 cup butter, 3/4 cup sugar, and the grated zest of 1 orange. When bubbly, dip biscuits into mixture and place upright in Bundt pan.

2. Cinnamon: Dip biscuits into a mixture of 1 cup sugar and 4 teaspoons cinnamon. Place in Bundt pan. Top with 1 cup pecans and 1/2 cup raisins, if desired. Drizzle 1/2 cup melted butter over all.

French Toast

Again, there are as many variations as there are kinds of bread. Go beyond white and wheat. Try sweet quick breads, such as zucchini, lemon, orange, poppy seed, banana nut, and pumpkin. Top with syrup or whipped cream. And try savory breads, such as onion, tomato, and garlic-herb. Top these with salsa and sour cream, like a Mexican omelet. Whenever we make regular French toast, we always stir cinnamon and vanilla into the egg mixture. Delicious!

Next time you have lemon, poppy seed, zucchini, or any other quick bread or pound cake on hand, use it to make French toast. Serve with a dusting of powdered sugar, a scoop of plump blueberries, and plenty of whipped cream.

Breakfast Packs

These are great for grabbing on the run. Pack each of these combinations in a resealable freezer bag, and you won't need to skip breakfast next time you're running late.

1. Homemade Ice Cream Sandwiches: *(See page 107.)* Use nutritious oatmeal-raisin cookies—or granola bars—and you have the equivalent of granola and cream.

2. Berries and Cheese: Freeze grapes or berries as explained on pages 17–18. Place them in small freezer bags with cubes of Monterey Jack cheese.

3. "Quick Bread" Sandwiches: Spread cream cheese between 2 slices of a fruit bread, such as cranberry or banana.

4. Ham and Cheese Rolls: Place a slice of cheese on a slice of ham, roll up and secure it with a wooden pick. Place 3 in each freezer bag, and freeze.

5. Pie Pockets: Make miniature pies of all kinds in muffin tins. Press pastry dough into muffin cup, fill with fruit or meat filling, then top with more pie pastry. Vent with a fork, bake, then freeze. Grab a pie as you leave and it will thaw before you get where you're going.

6. Pizza: You can grab a slice of pizza for a nutritious breakfast on the go.

7. Taquitos: Buy these already made and frozen, in bulk. Pack a few in a small freezer bag. (Look for miniature quiches and other hors d'oeuvres that can work the same way.) Just zap a few of them in the microwave and you'll have a hot, tasty breakfast in no time.

8. Crab or Salmon Cakes: When you make these *(see page 141),* make extra and freeze them for breakfast. They're great alone, or between two English muffins.

9. Quiches and Frittatas: When you make a large quiche or frittata, freeze a few individual wedges. Then, just heat in the microwave until heated through.

10. Quesadillas: The easiest way to make quesadillas is simply to melt cheese between 2 flour tortillas, in the microwave. Add whatever you wish—salsa, shredded cooked chicken, onions, olives, peppers, crab meat. Cut into serving sizes and freeze.

11. Snack Mixes: Don't forget trail-mix combinations, dried fruit packs, dry cereals, and other easy munchies.

12. Wraps: Next time you're frying up bacon, sausage, hash browns, or eggs, wrap some up in a flour tortilla. Secure with plastic wrap and freeze. When ready for a quick hand-held breakfast, heat one in the microwave for a minute or two, and off you go.

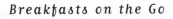

Nearly as easy as working with basic mixes is working with the recipes I've included for you in chapters 7 to 20. Chapter 7 presents your first week's menu of five main dishes that each serve four people. (Most of us have a couple of days a week when we eat on the run, or go out to dinner.)

Sometimes I suggest additional ideas to round out the menu, and with a few of the meals, I've thrown in some of my favorite (and easiest) dessert recipes. This method is even easier than working with basic mixes, because all you have to do is warm up the cooked dinners!

During each week you'll cook multiple portions of some items; these will appear in two or more of that week's recipes. Cooking in quantity not only saves you time and money, but also makes your cooking day easier.

These recipes are far more varied than those created using mixes. These creations will tantalize your taste buds and make every evening meal a dinner you can look forward to. Now let's get started. And don't forget to select one of the meals to have for dinner tonight.

week one

Menu

Soup

California Cream of Spinach Soup

Main Dishes

Fajita Salad with Goat Cheese

Peaches and Cream Stuffed Pork Chops

Quick Curry Quiche with Fresh Mango Chutney

Spinach Fettuccine with Goat Cheese and Bacon

Tandoori Chicken with Couscous

Desserts

Georgia Peach Ice Cream Pie

Papaya Sherbet

shopping list

The following list is exactly what you'll need for the week's dinners. Obviously you can't buy each item in the indicated quantity, but use this list to shop accordingly. Do an inventory of your cupboards and refrigerator before shopping, and **purchase only the items you don't already have.** The quantities listed here are for use in this week's menus only; in some cases you'll need to buy more of certain items than you need for the week: you may need to buy a bottle of spice, for example, only to use a small amount. But you'll use more in subsequent weeks.

BAKING MIXES AND FLOURS

1 cup buttermilk baking mix
1 tablespoon cornstarch
1 can (14 ounces) evaporated milk

BREADS AND GRAINS/PASTA/RICE

2 cornbread muffins or cornbread slices
1 prepared graham cracker piecrust
1 cup uncooked couscous
16 ounces (1 pound) spinach fettuccine

CHEESE/DAIRY/EGGS

12 ounces goat cheese
2 1/2 cups grated jalapeño Monterey Jack cheese
freshly grated Parmesan cheese to taste (about 1/4 cup)
1/3 cup ricotta cheese
2 cups half-and-half
1/2 gallon vanilla bean ice cream
2 cups milk
1/2 cup nonfat sour cream
1/2 cup lime yogurt
7 eggs

CONDIMENTS AND SAUCES

6 tablespoon-cubes frozen white sauce, or 3 tablespoons each butter and flour

FLAVORINGS/HERBS*/ SEASONINGS/SPICES

2 teaspoons dried basil
3/4 teaspoon cinnamon
1/4 teaspoon ground coriander
1/4 teaspoon ground cumin
1 teaspoon curry powder
1 envelope (1.25 ounces) fajita seasoning mix
1/4 teaspoon garlic powder
1/4 teaspoon ground ginger
1/2 teaspoon nutmeg
1/4 teaspoon paprika
1/4 teaspoon red (cayenne) pepper
1/2 teaspoon poultry seasoning
Salt and pepper
2 tablespoons sesame seeds
1 teaspoon vanilla

FRUITS/NUTS/VEGETABLES

3 kiwi
Juice of 1 lime
1 cup diced bottled mango
2 papayas (or 1 pound bottled papaya)
2 cups fresh, frozen, or canned sliced peaches
3/4 cup raisins
1 can (15 ounces) black beans
1 1/2 cups fresh or frozen sliced carrots
1 can (15 ounces) chickpeas (garbanzo beans)
2 tablespoons chopped cilantro

1 teaspoon fresh or bottled minced garlic
1 jar or can (4 ounces) sliced mushrooms
2 teaspoons minced onion
5 cups fresh or frozen chopped onion
2 tablespoons chopped fresh parsley
2 tablespoons chopped red onion
1 jar (10 ounces) roasted red peppers (2 cups)
4 cups mixed salad greens
2 packages (10 ounces each) frozen chopped spinach
4 yellow crookneck squash

LIQUIDS

2 1/4 cups chicken stock or broth

MEAT/SEAFOOD

1 pound bacon (14 slices)
10 boneless, skinless, split chicken breasts
4 pork loin chops (1 inch thick)

OILS

1 tablespoon olive oil
5 tablespoons vegetable or olive oil

SWEETS AND SWEETENERS

1 can (6 ounces) frozen fruit juice concentrate (try an exotic blend, such as guava mango or passion fruit pineapple)
1/2 cup peach jam
1/3 cup plus 1 tablespoon plus 1 teaspoon sugar

*If using fresh herbs, double the amount listed here.

PUTTING IT ALL TOGETHER

1. Thaw 6 tablespoon-cubes of frozen white sauce mix, or mix 3 tablespoons of flour with 3 tablespoons of butter in a small bowl, using a pastry blender, fork, or two knives. Set aside.

2. Thaw spinach, carrots (if frozen), ice cream, fruit juice concentrate, and chicken stock (if frozen).

3. Sauté the chicken in 5 tablespoons oil, in a Dutch oven or large nonstick stockpot or skillet, for 10 minutes per side, or until chicken is no longer pink inside. Remove from heat.

4. Cook the pork chops in the microwave until done, about 10 minutes.

5. Dice peaches.

6. Peel and dice kiwi.

7. Cut up bacon into 1-inch strips, fry, and drain on paper towels. Using the bacon drippings, sauté chopped onion until transparent. Drain, but reserve the drippings.

8. Boil water in a large saucepan; cook the fettuccine. Drain.

9. Grate Jack cheese (if not already grated).

10. Cut 2 of the yellow squash into 2-inch strips; slice and halve the other two.

11. Slice roasted red peppers.

12. Butter a 10-inch pie plate for Quick Curry Quiche.

13. Peel and slice the papaya.

As you pull out the ingredients and cooking pots to do your once-a-week cooking, just remind yourself that you used to do this every day—amazing!

TIP:

Cut bacon up with kitchen shears before you fry it. The bacon cooks faster and more evenly.

Using everything you have just prepared, create these simple, tasty dishes.

soup

California Cream of Spinach Soup

6	tablespoon-cubes frozen white sauce, or 3 tablespoons each butter and flour, combined
1/2	cup sautéed chopped onion
2	packages (10 ounces each) frozen chopped spinach, thawed and squeezed dry *(see variation)*
1/4	cup chicken stock or broth
2	cups half-and-half
	Salt and pepper to taste
1	cup grated jalapeño Monterey Jack cheese
8	slices bacon, chopped and cooked

Place white sauce cubes (or combined butter and flour), onion, and spinach in a nonstick soup pot over medium-low heat. Stir until mixture melts. Reduce heat to simmer. Blend in stock, half-and-half, and salt and pepper. Simmer only—do not boil. Serve in four large bowls, sprinkled with Jack cheese and bacon.

VARIATION: Because not everyone is a spinach lover, try making this soup with chopped broccoli or asparagus.

main dishes

Fajita Salad with Goat Cheese

1	tablespoon olive oil
1	envelope (1.25 ounces) fajita seasoning mix
2	yellow crookneck squash, cut into 2-inch strips
1/2	cup sautéed chopped onion
1	can (15 ounces) black beans, drained
1	jar or can (4 ounces) sliced mushrooms
1	cup roasted red peppers, sliced
4	boneless, skinless, split chicken breasts, cooked
1/2	cup nonfat sour cream
1/2	cup lime yogurt
4	ounces goat cheese, crumbled
4	cups mixed salad greens

In a large skillet over medium heat, stir olive oil, fajita seasoning mix, squash, onion, black beans, and mushrooms. When squash is tender, add roasted red peppers and immediately remove from heat.

Cube chicken and place in a large bowl. Add vegetable mixture, sour cream, and lime yogurt. Stir until thoroughly combined. Add goat cheese. Refrigerate for 30 minutes, then freeze in four portions.

When ready to serve, thaw in refrigerator, then stir over medium heat in saucepan until heated through. Serve hot over salad greens. This dish may also be served cold.

VARIATION: Another great way to enjoy this chicken fajita dish is to serve it over pasta or a baked potato instead of salad greens.

TIP:

Sliced lettuce doesn't brown any more quickly than torn lettuce. Make your salad faster by using kitchen shears.

Peaches and Cream Stuffed Pork Chops

1	cup diced fresh peaches
2	cornbread muffins (or two thick slices cornbread), crumbled
1/3	cup ricotta cheese
1/3	cup sugar
1	egg, beaten
2	teaspoons minced onion
1/2	teaspoon poultry seasoning
1/2	teaspoon nutmeg
4	pork loin chops, 1-inch thick, with slit cut in edge opposite rib bone to form pocket
1/2	cup peach jam
	Salt and pepper to taste

Preheat oven to 350 degrees F. In a large bowl, mix peaches, muffins, ricotta cheese, sugar, egg, onion, poultry seasoning, and nutmeg. Stuff a spoonful into each of the four pork chop pockets (you will have extra stuffing left). Press chops to close and place in a 9 × 13-inch baking dish. Spread jam over chops. Sprinkle with salt and pepper.

Place excess stuffing in a separate buttered baking dish. Bake both dishes for 30 minutes.

Cool both dishes quickly, then freeze. Remember, these chops will be slightly undercooked, and you will cook them a little more upon reheating.

When ready to serve, heat in microwave for 10 minutes if frozen or 6 minutes if thawed. Or heat, covered, in regular oven for 45 minutes if frozen or 25 minutes if thawed.

VARIATION: Try apples if you prefer them to peaches. Also, you can use chicken or lamb instead of pork.

Serving Suggestion: Serve with steamed, parsleyed new potatoes and California Cream of Spinach Soup (see page 58).

Quick Curry Quiche with Fresh Mango Chutney

2	reserved portions Tandoori Chicken with Couscous *(see page 63)*
1 1/2	cups grated jalapeño Monterey Jack cheese
2	cups milk
1	cup buttermilk baking mix
6	eggs

Preheat oven to 425 degrees F. In a large bowl, stir together all ingredients. Turn into buttered pie plate. Bake for 30 minutes. Chill, then wrap tightly and freeze.

When ready to serve, bake at 350 degrees F for 45 minutes, or thaw first and bake, covered, for 30 minutes. Slice into wedges and serve topped with fresh mango chutney *(see recipe below)*.

Serving Suggestion: Slices of melon are good on the side.

Fresh Mango Chutney

1	cup diced bottled mango
3	kiwi, peeled and diced
2	tablespoons chopped red onion
2	tablespoons chopped cilantro
	Juice of 1 lime

Mix all ingredients in a medium-size bowl and serve.

Spinach Fettuccine with Goat Cheese and Bacon

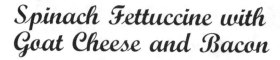

2	tablespoons bacon drippings
6	slices bacon, chopped and cooked
2	yellow crookneck squash, sliced and halved
1	cup roasted red peppers, sliced
1	teaspoon fresh or bottled minced garlic
2	teaspoons dried basil (or 4 teaspoons fresh)
16	ounces (1 pound) spinach fettuccine, cooked and drained
	Freshly grated Parmesan cheese to taste (about 1/4 cup)
8	ounces goat cheese, crumbled
	Salt and pepper to taste

In a large skillet, heat bacon drippings over medium heat. Add bacon, squash slices, red peppers, garlic, and basil. Sauté until squash is just tender. Toss with cooked fettuccine. When cool, add cheeses, salt, and pepper. Freeze in four portions.

When ready to serve, thaw and then heat in covered dish in oven for 40 minutes at 350 degrees, or in microwave for 10 minutes. This may also be heated in the top of a double boiler.

VARIATION: Substitute other crumbly cheeses for goat cheese.

Serving Suggestion: Serve with a colorful salad of fresh, seasonal fruit.

Tandoori Chicken with Couscous

6	boneless, skinless, split chicken breasts, cooked and sliced
1/4	teaspoon garlic powder
1/4	teaspoon cinnamon
1/4	teaspoon ground ginger
1/4	teaspoon ground coriander
1/4	teaspoon ground cumin
1/4	teaspoon paprika
1/4	teaspoon red (cayenne) pepper
1 1/2	cups sautéed chopped onion
1 1/2	cups fresh or frozen sliced carrots
3/4	cup raisins
2	tablespoons sesame seeds
2	tablespoons chopped fresh parsley
1	tablespoon cornstarch
2	cups chicken stock or broth

Place all ingredients in a Dutch oven or large nonstick skillet. Simmer for 10 minutes. Serve over Curried Chickpea Couscous.

Curried Chickpea Couscous

1	cup uncooked couscous
1	can (15 ounces) chickpeas (garbanzo beans), drained
1	teaspoon curry powder

While the Tandoori Chicken is simmering, prepare couscous according to package directions, but add chickpeas and curry powder to the water.

This recipe makes 6 portions, so reserve one-fourth of both the chicken mixture and the couscous, and use them in preparing Quick Curry Quiche *(see recipe on page 61)*. Freeze the rest in four portions, with the couscous frozen separately from the chicken mixture.

Thaw in refrigerator or in top of double boiler. Heat on stove top for 5 to 10 minutes, stirring over simmering heat; or heat in oven, covered, for 30 minutes at 350 degrees F; or heat for 7 minutes in microwave oven. This makes a complete meal, but if you wish, add a crisp green salad and fresh bread.

VARIATION: Try rice in place of couscous.

TIP:

Instead of combining multiple spices to make Tandoori, southwest, Thai, or Caribbean seasoning rubs, look for ready-made ethnic blends in the spice aisle of your favorite market.

Couscous is the new "rice," but actually it's a super fast-cooking pasta. It's showing up in all kinds of dishes, not just exotic ones. Check the rice and grains aisle at your market for easy and different side dishes— try bulgur, wheat, polenta, and barley.

desserts

Georgia Peach Ice Cream Pie

1/2	gallon vanilla bean ice cream, thawed
1	can (6 ounces) frozen fruit juice concentrate, thawed
1/2	teaspoon cinnamon
1/2	teaspoon sugar
1	cup diced peaches
1	prepared graham cracker piecrust

Mix ice cream with frozen juice concentrate. Mix cinnamon and sugar with peaches, then add to ice cream mixture. Spoon into piecrust and freeze. It doesn't get any easier than this!

VARIATION: Make a gingersnap crumb crust instead of using a graham cracker crust. Preheat oven to 350 degrees F. Whirl gingersnaps in a blender or food processor until you have 1 1/2 cups of crumbs. Mix with 3 tablespoons sugar and 1/3 cup butter. Press into pie plate and bake for 10 minutes. Cool. Fill with ice cream mixture and freeze.

The Once-a-Week Cookbook

Papaya Sherbet

1	can (14 ounces) evaporated milk
2	papayas (or 1 pound bottled papaya)
1	tablespoon sugar
1	teaspoon vanilla

Pour milk into a plastic container, cover and freeze. Purée papaya in blender or food processor. Beat frozen milk in the bowl of an electric mixer with sugar and vanilla until fluffy. Fold in puréed papaya. Freeze. Beat and freeze once again before serving.

VARIATION: Substitute peaches for papayas.

If you feel like getting fancy, serve this fun sherbet in hollowed out papaya halves or coconuts.

CHAPTER EIGHT

week two

Soup

Ruby Poached Pear Soup

Salad

Chilled Bean Salad

Main Dishes

Easy Cioppino

Maple-Glazed Salmon

Orange Blossom Salmon Stir-Fry

Southern Shrimp au Gratin

Seafood Enchiladas

Desserts

Bonbon Wontons

Chewy Caramel Oatmeal Bars

shopping list

This week is for the seafood-loving household; however, if you're not crazy about seafood, simply substitute pork or chicken in any of these recipies. The following list is exactly what you'll need for the week's dinners, so shop accordingly. *You need only purchase those items you don't already have on hand.*

....

**BAKING MIXES
AND FLOURS**
1/2 teaspoon baking soda
2 cups all-purpose flour

**BREADS AND
GRAINS/PASTA/RICE**
1 cup old-fashioned oats
2 dozen flour tortillas
    (10 inches each)
16 square wonton wrappers
4 cups uncooked rice or pasta

CHEESE/DAIRY/EGGS
4 ounces blue cheese
1/2 pound grated Cheddar cheese
1 pound grated Colby-Jack cheese
    (or mix Jack and Cheddar)
1 3/4 cups (3 sticks) butter
1 can (13 ounces) evaporated milk
1 cup sour cream
2 eggs

CONDIMENTS AND SAUCES
1 can (16 ounces) enchilada sauce
1/4 cup honey-mustard salad
    dressing
1 tablespoon soy sauce
3 tablespoons balsamic vinegar
16 tablespoon-cubes frozen white
    sauce, or 8 tablespoons each
    butter and flour

**FLAVORINGS/HERBS*/
SEASONINGS/SPICES**
1/4 teaspoon allspice
1/4 teaspoon ground black pepper

1 teaspoon red (cayenne) pepper
1/2 teaspoon red pepper flakes
Salt and pepper
3 tablespoons sesame seeds

**FRUITS/NUTS/
VEGETABLES**
Juice of 1 lemon
1 tablespoon grated orange rind
1 pound pears, peeled and
    chopped (may use canned)
1/2 cup nuts (pecans, walnuts,
    or macadamia nuts)
1 jar (10 ounces) artichoke hearts
1 can (15 ounces) black beans
1 can (8.75 ounces) garbanzo
    beans
1 can (8.75 ounces) kidney beans
1 can (15 ounces) mixed green
    and wax beans
1 can (16 ounces) sliced beets
1 can (4 ounces) chopped mild
    green chilies
1 can (16 ounces) miniature corn
    on the cob
1 1/2 teaspoons crushed garlic
Fresh ginger to grate (1 table-
    spoon), or 1 teaspoon ground
    ginger
1 can (4 ounces) chopped black
    olives
6 1/2 cups fresh or frozen
    chopped onion
1/2 cup diced red onion
1 red bell pepper

1 jar (8 ounces) roasted red
    peppers
1 package (14 ounces) frozen stir-
    fry vegetables (or use fresh)
2 cans (15 ounces each) Italian
    stewed tomatoes

LIQUIDS
2 cups chicken stock or broth
1 bottle (8 ounces) clam juice
2 tablespoons orange juice

MEAT/SEAFOOD
8 salmon steaks, cut 1-inch thick
3 pounds mixed seafood: sea
    bass, scallops, mussels, crab,
    or your favorites
1 1/2 pounds fresh or frozen
    shrimp (may substitute
    chicken or crab for 1 pound
    of the shrimp)

OILS
3 tablespoons olive oil
2 cups plus 3 tablespoons
    vegetable oil

SWEETS AND SWEETENERS
3/4 cup caramel ice cream topping
8 creme-filled chocolate candies
1 package (6 ounces) semisweet
    chocolate chips
2 tablespoons molasses
1/2 cup maple syrup
3/4 cup brown sugar
1/3 cup powdered sugar
1 tablespoon sugar

*If using fresh herbs, double the amount listed here.

PUTTING IT ALL TOGETHER

1. Freeze the candies.

2. Thaw 16 tablespoon-cubes of frozen white sauce mix, or mix 8 tablespoons each of flour and butter into a paste.

3. In a large skillet, heat 3 tablespoons vegetable oil. Sauté the frozen chopped onion until transparent. Drain. (You will have some cooked onion left over for later use.)

4. Peel shrimp if necessary. Wash all seafood.

5. Grate cheese (if not already grated).

6. If you'll want rice or pasta with any of the dishes, prepare it according to package instructions.

7. Butter a 9 × 13-inch baking dish for Maple-Glazed Salmon and a 9-inch square baking dish for Chewy Caramel Oatmeal Bars.

8. Grate orange rind, then squeeze juice into a cup.

9. Slice salmon into 1/2-inch wide strips.

Using everything you have just prepared, create these simple, tasty dishes.

soup

Ruby Poached Pear Soup

3/4	cup sautéed chopped onion
1	can (16 ounces) sliced beets, with juice
1	pound pears, peeled and chopped (may use canned)
1/4	teaspoon allspice
1/4	teaspoon ground black pepper
2	cups chicken stock or broth
4	ounces blue cheese, crumbled

In a blender or food processor fitted with a metal blade, purée onion, beets, pears, allspice, and pepper. Stir in broth. Freeze in four portions.
When ready to serve, heat in saucepan over low heat until simmering. Ladle into bowls and top each serving with blue cheese.

NOTE: This festive soup is bright pink.

TIP:

Garlic peels slip off easily if you first microwave the garlic for ten seconds.

salad

Chilled Bean Salad

1	can (15 ounces) black beans, drained
1	can (8.75 ounces) garbanzo beans, drained
1	can (8.75 ounces) kidney beans, drained
1	can (15 ounces) mixed green and wax beans, drained
1	red bell pepper, diced
1/2	cup diced red onion
3	tablespoons balsamic vinegar
3	tablespoons olive oil
1	tablespoon sugar
1/2	teaspoon red pepper flakes
	Salt and pepper to taste

Toss all ingredients together in a large bowl. Divide into serving portions and freeze.

When ready to serve, thaw in refrigerator. Stir and served chilled.

TIP:

When chopping onions, cut the root end off last. It will hold the slices together for cross-cutting, and reduce tears to boot. Chilling an onion also reduces tears.

main dishes

Easy Cioppino

1	cup sautéed chopped onion
1 1/2	teaspoons crushed garlic
1	jar (8 ounces) roasted red peppers, chopped
2	cans (15 ounces each) Italian stewed tomatoes
1	bottle (8 ounces) clam juice
1/4	teaspoon red (cayenne) pepper
2	salmon steaks, cut into chunks
1/2	pound shrimp
1	pound mixed seafood
	Salt and pepper to taste

In a large stockpot, combine all ingredients. Cook over medium heat for 3 minutes, adjust seasonings, then freeze in 4 to 6 portions.

When ready to serve, warm just until heated through and seafood is opaque.

Serving Suggestions: Serve in soup bowls alone, over rice, or with cooked pasta. Crusty rolls or focaccia bread and thyme-seasoned butter are a wonderful accompaniment. Simply stir a teaspoon of crushed thyme into a softened stick of butter.

For dessert, crumble the reserved Chewy Caramel Oatmeal Bars (see page 78) over bowls of vanilla ice cream.

Maple-Glazed Salmon

4	salmon steaks, cut 1-inch thick
6	tablespoons butter, softened
1/4	teaspoon red (cayenne) pepper
	Water
	Juice of 1 lemon
1/2	cup maple syrup

Preheat oven to 300 degrees F. Place the salmon in buttered baking dish. In a small bowl, mix butter with cayenne pepper; spread over steaks. Pour water in baking dish to depth of 1/2-inch around steaks. Add lemon juice to water. Bake uncovered for 10 minutes. Pour maple syrup over each steak. Bake another 5 minutes, or until centers of salmon steaks are still pink and raw, while edges are beginning to turn opaque. Chill quickly, wrap tightly in foil, and freeze.

When ready to serve, thaw in refrigerator, then warm in oven at 275 degrees F for 10 minutes.

VARIATION: Substitute other kinds of fish for salmon.

Serving Suggestion: Serve with wild rice, asparagus, and Ruby Poached Pear Soup (see page 70).

NOTE: Overcooked salmon cannot be salvaged. Be sure to undercook these steaks so that warming them up does not dry them out.

Orange Blossom Salmon Stir-Fry

1/4	cup honey-mustard salad dressing
3	tablespoons sesame seeds
2	tablespoons molasses
2	tablespoons orange juice
1	tablespoon soy sauce
1	tablespoon fresh ground ginger or 1 teaspoon powdered ginger
1	tablespoon grated orange rind
1	package (14 ounces) frozen stir-fry vegetables
2	salmon steaks, sliced into 1/2-inch strips
4	cups cooked rice or pasta

In a large skillet over medium heat, combine salad dressing, sesame seeds, molasses, orange juice, soy sauce, ginger, and orange rind. Add vegetables and salmon, stirring until vegetables are tender-crisp and salmon is not quite opaque. Remove from heat and place in freezer container(s). Freeze.

When ready to serve, thaw in top of double boiler, or bake frozen in covered 9 × 13-inch dish at 325 degrees F for 25 minutes, or until heated through and fish is opaque. Serve over rice or pasta.

VARIATION: Remove the salmon for a delicious vegetarian dish. Or, if you're not crazy about seafood, substitute chicken, lamb, or beef for salmon.

Southern Shrimp au Gratin

1	cup (or 16) thawed white sauce tablespoon-cubes, or 1 1/2 cup each butter and flour, combined
1	can (13 ounces) evaporated milk
	Additional milk, or half-and-half (if needed to thin sauce, use up to 1 cup)
2	egg yolks, beaten
1/2	teaspoon red (cayenne) pepper
1	pound peeled, fresh or frozen shrimp (may substitute chicken or crab)
1	jar (10 ounces) artichoke hearts, drained
1	can (16 ounces) miniature corn on the cob, drained
1	cup sautéed chopped onion
	Salt and pepper to taste
1/2	pound grated Cheddar cheese

In a large skillet over medium-low heat, melt white sauce cubes or flour and butter mixture. Increase heat to medium. Stir in milk or half-and-half and yolks until thick sauce forms. Add additional milk or half-and-half if sauce is too thick. Stir in red pepper, shrimp, artichoke hearts, miniature corn, onion, salt, and pepper. Adjust seasonings. Freeze.

When ready to serve, thaw in refrigerator, then bake in 9 × 13-inch casserole dish at 375 degrees F for 10 to 15 minutes (half again as long if casserole goes directly from freezer to oven). Sprinkle with cheese during last 5 minutes of baking.

Serving Suggestion: Serve over cooked rice or pasta, with glossy green beans or broccoli on the side.

Seafood Enchiladas

1/2	cup sautéed chopped onion
1	can (4 ounces) chopped olives
1	can (4 ounces) chopped mild green chilies
1	can (16 ounces) enchilada sauce
1	cup sour cream
2	dozen flour tortillas
2	pounds mixed seafood (white fish, shrimp, lobster, crab, mussels, scallops as desired—even tuna)
1	pound grated Colby-Jack cheese (or mix Jack and Cheddar)

In a large bowl, combine onion, olives, chilies, enchilada sauce, and sour cream. Dip each tortilla into this mixture, then roll up 1/2 cup seafood with a pinch of cheese inside each tortilla. Place in a 9 × 13-inch baking dish. (It's messy, but worth it.) Pour remaining sauce over enchiladas, then cover with remaining grated cheese. Freeze.

When ready to serve, thaw in refrigerator and bake at 350 degrees F for 15 minutes. Or, bake directly from freezer for 30 minutes, or until cheese is bubbly.

VARIATION: Spanish rice makes a good side dish. Just mix a jar of salsa with 4 cups cooked rice.

Serving Suggestion: Serve with Chilled Bean Salad (see page 71).

desserts

Bonbon Wontons

1 to 2	cups vegetable oil
16	square wonton wrappers
8	frozen creme-filled chocolate candies
1/3	cup powdered sugar

Heat 1 inch of oil in a medium skillet over medium-high heat, until it sizzles a drop of water. Place a frozen candy on each of 8 wonton wrappers. Working quickly, moisten remaining 8 wrappers and cover bonbons, pressing to seal edges of wrappers. Fry in oil, turning frequently, for about 30 seconds, until wrappers are golden. Drain on paper towels. Dust with powdered sugar and serve at once.

VARIATION: Use an ice cream bonbon instead of a frozen candy one. The only difference is that you'll have to work a little faster, as the ice cream melts quickly. They're messier to eat, but definitely delicious!

"We dare not trust our wit for making our house pleasant to our friend, so we buy ice cream."

—Ralph Waldo Emerson

Chewy Caramel Oatmeal Bars

1	cup plus 3 tablespoons all-purpose flour
1	cup old-fashioned oats
3/4	cup brown sugar
1/2	teaspoon baking soda
3/4	cup (1 1/2 sticks) butter, melted
1	package (6 ounces) semisweet chocolate chips
1/2	cup nuts (pecans, walnuts, or macadamia nuts)
3/4	cup caramel ice cream topping

Preheat oven to 350 degrees F. Reserve 3 tablespoons of flour. In a medium bowl, using a fork or spoon, thoroughly mix flour, oats, brown sugar, and baking soda with melted butter. Divide oatmeal mixture in half. Press half of mixture onto bottom of buttered baking dish. Bake for 8 to 10 minutes, until golden. Sprinkle chocolate chips and nuts over warm crust.

In a small bowl, combine reserved flour with caramel topping and drizzle over the nuts. Top with remaining oatmeal mixture and bake for another 15 to 20 minutes. Chill before cutting. Wrap tightly and freeze.

Reserve a third of the bars for Cioppino night. *(See page 72.)*

VARIATION: Substitute butterscotch chips for chocolate chips.

week three

Menu

Soup

Wild Rice Soup Alfredo

Main Dishes

Taos Taco Salad

Barbecued Beef Quiche with Cool Pineapple Salsa

Beef Wellingtons Béarnaise

Buck Island Beef with Ginger Pear Salsa

Muffin Cup Meat Loaves

Side Dishes

Key Lime Pie Bread

San Antonio Rice

Desserts

Chocolate Peanut Butter Pie

Frozen Dessert Pops

shopping list

The following list is exactly what you'll need for the week's dinners, so shop accordingly. You need only purchase those items you don't already have on hand.

BAKING MIXES AND FLOURS

1/2 cup buttermilk baking mix
1 teaspoon baking soda
1 3/4 cups all-purpose flour

BREADS AND GRAINS/PASTA/RICE

2 baked piecrusts, or 2 graham cracker crusts
5 cups seasoned stuffing mix
4 cups taco-flavored tortilla chips
48 (4-inch) wonton wrappers
2 cups uncooked seasoned long grain wild rice
4 cups uncooked wild or white rice

CHEESE/DAIRY/EGGS

1/2 cup crumbled blue cheese
2 1/2 cups grated Cheddar cheese

2 packages (8 ounces each) cream cheese
5 cups grated Monterey Jack cheese (3 cups may be jalapeño Jack)
1 cup (2 sticks) butter
2 cups half-and-half
4 cups plus 3 tablespoons milk
2 cups low-fat sour cream
1 carton (8 ounces) vanilla yogurt
1 cup frozen whipped topping, or 1 cup whipped cream
1 cup whipping cream
16 eggs

CONDIMENTS AND SAUCES

3/4 cup bottled barbecue sauce
1/4 cup ketchup
1 1/4 cup peanut butter

1 bottle (16 ounces or 1 pint) Russian salad dressing
6 tablespoon-cubes frozen white sauce, or 3 tablespoons each butter and flour
2 tablespoons Worcestershire sauce

FLAVORINGS/HERBS*/ SEASONINGS/SPICES

1 package (0.9 ounce) béarnaise sauce mix
2 tablespoons plus 1/2 teaspoon Caribbean Jerk Seasoning[†]
2/3 cup plus 2 teaspoons fresh cilantro
1/4 teaspoon garlic salt
1/4 teaspoon dry mustard
1/2 teaspoon red pepper flakes
1/4 teaspoon sage

*If using fresh herbs, double the amount listed here.
[†]I rarely recommend a particular brand name, but you *must* have a jar of Schilling/McCormick Caribbean Jerk Seasoning in your pantry.

Salt and pepper
1 tablespoon vanilla

FRUITS/NUTS/
VEGETABLES
Juice of 1 lime plus
  1/3 cup lime juice[††]
1/4 cup lemon juice
1 banana
2 Bartlett pears
1 can (6 ounces) crushed
  pineapple
3 cups fresh or frozen
  strawberries
1/4 teaspoon coconut extract
1 can (15 ounces) black or
  kidney beans
1 can (15 ounces) black
  beans
1 can (5 ounces) chopped
  mild green, chipotle,
  or jalapeño chilies
1 cucumber

1 teaspoon grated fresh
  ginger
1 head lettuce
1 cup sliced canned or fresh
  mushrooms
1 can (15 ounces) sliced
  olives
5 cups fresh or frozen
  chopped onion
1 red onion
3 tomatoes

LIQUIDS
4 cups (or 3 cans) chicken
  stock or broth
1 cup orange juice
3/4 cup grape juice

MEAT/SEAFOOD
9 (6 ounces each) boneless
  beef rib eye or tenderloin
  steaks, cut 3/4-inch thick
1/2 pound ground sausage
2 pounds ground sirloin

OILS
1 cup plus 2 tablespoons
  vegetable oil

SWEETS AND
SWEETENERS
1 cup applesauce
1 package (6 ounces) semisweet
  chocolate chips
12 to 16 miniature chocolate
  peanut butter cups
1 package (3.4 ounces) instant
  vanilla pudding
1 package (3.4 ounces) chocolate
  pudding
Magic Shell chocolate ice
  cream topping (optional)
1 cup superfine sugar
2 3/4 cups plus 2 tablespoons
  and 1 teaspoon sugar

MISCELLANEOUS
Plastic pop molds for Frozen
  Dessert Pops

[††]You can buy bottled key lime juice (at my store it's even less expensive than regular lime juice). Key limes are lighter in color and mellower in flavor. If unavailable, just squeeze some fresh lime juice.

PUTTING IT ALL TOGETHER

1. Thaw 6 tablespoon-cubes of frozen white sauce mix, or mix 3 tablespoons each of flour and butter into a paste.
2. Thaw strawberries (if using frozen) and whipped topping.
3. Soften cream cheese.
4. In a large saucepan, cook the wild or white rice.
5. In a medium saucepan, cook the seasoned long grain wild rice.
6. In a large skillet, sauté the chopped white onions in 2 tablespoons vegetable oil. Cut the red onion in half. Dice one half and mince the other half.
7. Chop cilantro.
8. Cook sausage until browned and crumbly; drain.
9. Cook one of the pounds of ground sirloin until crumbly; drain.
10. Prepare stuffing: In a large bowl, mix sausage, 2 cups chicken stock or broth, 5 cups dry seasoned stuffing, sliced mushrooms, 1/2 cup sautéed onions. Freeze all but two cups.

11. Grease and flour a loaf pan for Key Lime Pie Bread. Butter a 10-inch quiche or pie plate for Barbecued Beef Quiche and a 9 × 13-inch baking dish for San Antonio Rice.
12. Cut 4 of the steaks into 1-inch cubes.
13. Grate cheese (if not already grated).
14. Make Frozen Dessert Pops.
15. Crush tortilla chips.

The Once-a-Week Cookbook

Using everything you have just prepared, create these simple, tasty dishes.

soup

Wild Rice Soup Alfredo

2	cups cooked seasoned long grain wild rice
1	cup sautéed chopped onion
2	cups chicken stock or broth
6	tablespoon-cubes white sauce, thawed, or 3 tablespoons each butter and flour, combined
2	cups half-and-half (use half milk for lower-fat version)
	Salt and pepper to taste

In a large soup pot over low heat, combine all ingredients and simmer until half-and-half is thickened by white sauce cubes or butter and flour combination. Quick chill, then freeze.

When ready to serve, reheat in top of double boiler until hot but not boiling.

VARIATIONS: Stir in a cup of corn, chopped asparagus, sliced mushrooms, or grated Jarlsberg cheese. Or, make it a killer main dish by adding 2 cups of cooked shrimp or flaked salmon. Leftover cooked rice can be mixed with vegetables for a side dish. Or, use it in your next stuffing, meat loaf, casserole, or in crab cakes.

TIP:
Snip herbs with scissors instead of mincing with a knife—much simpler and safer.

main dishes

Taos Taco Salad

1	pound cooked and crumbled ground sirloin
1/2	red onion, diced
1 1/2	cups grated Cheddar cheese
1	can (15 ounces) sliced olives
1	can (15 ounces) black or kidney beans, drained
3	tomatoes, diced
1/3	cup chopped cilantro
5	cups shredded lettuce
4	cups taco-flavored tortilla chips, crushed
1	bottle (16 ounces or 1 pint) Russian salad dressing

In a large bowl, combine ground sirloin, red onion, cheese, olives, and beans. Freeze.

When ready to serve, thaw in refrigerator, then toss with tomatoes, cilantro, lettuce, tortilla chips, and Russian dressing.

VARIATION: Try chicken or fish instead of sirloin.

Serving Suggestion: Serve with San Antonio Rice (see page 92).

NOTE: Perfect for a party—just double or triple the recipe.

Barbecued Beef Quiche with Cool Pineapple Salsa

1	rib eye or tenderloin steak reserved from Buck Island recipe *(see page 89)*, cubed (about 1 1/2 cups)
3/4	cup store-bought barbecue sauce
2	cups grated Monterey Jack cheese
1/2	cup minced red onion
8	eggs
1	cup milk
1/2	cup buttermilk baking mix
	Salt and pepper to taste

Preheat oven to 400 degrees F. In a large bowl, combine beef with barbecue sauce, cheese, and red onion. Pour into buttered quiche or pie plate. In another bowl, whisk eggs, milk, baking mix, salt, and pepper until well mixed. Pour over beef mixture. Bake for 40 minutes (it won't be quite done). Quick cool, then wrap tightly and freeze.

When ready to serve, thaw in refrigerator or oven (remember to cook it longer if quiche goes directly from freezer to oven). Bake at 400 degrees F for 10 minutes, or until knife inserted in center comes out clean.

Cool Pineapple Salsa

1	can (6 ounces) crushed pineapple, drained (reserve juice)
1	cucumber, peeled and chopped
1/3	cup chopped cilantro
1/2	teaspoon Caribbean Jerk Seasoning

While quiche bakes, prepare salsa. In a medium bowl, combine all ingredients Top each wedge of quiche with this salsa.

Serving Suggestion: Coleslaw makes a wonderful side dish.

TIP:

To ensure brown gravy, "toast" some flour in an ovenproof mug, right alongside your roast. When the meat is done, the flour is ready, too.

Beef Wellingtons Béarnaise

4	(6 ounces each) beef rib eye or tenderloin steaks, cut into 1-inch cubes
1	package (0.9 ounce) béarnaise sauce mix
48	(4-inch) wonton wrappers
1	cup cooking oil

In a resealable plastic bag, toss meat with dry béarnaise sauce mix until well coated. Place each cube of meat on a wonton wrapper, then moisten the edges of another wrapper and seal it over the meat. This will make 24. Freeze.

When ready to serve, thaw in refrigerator. Fry in skillet of hot oil (half an inch deep) until golden, about 5 minutes per side. Turn with tongs, and drain on paper towels. Serves 6 per person.

Serving Suggestion: These also make great appetizers, but as a main dish, serve with shiny, stir-fried vegetables and a refreshing green salad with balsamic vinegar dressing.

Buck Island Beef with Ginger Pear Salsa

2	tablespoons Caribbean Jerk Seasoning*
5	boneless beef rib eye or tenderloin steaks, cut 3/4 inch thick

Heat broiler. Press Jerk Seasoning into both sides of steaks. Broil steaks 2 to 3 inches from heat for 7 to 10 minutes, turning once. Remove from broiler while still rare. Reserve one of the steaks for Barbecued Beef Quiche *(see page 87)*, then quick chill, wrap, and freeze the others.

When ready to serve, thaw in refrigerator, then finish broiling until meat reaches desired level of doneness.

Ginger Pear Salsa

2	Bartlett pears, peeled and diced
1/2	cup crumbled blue cheese
	Juice of 1 lime
1	teaspoon grated fresh ginger
2	teaspoons chopped cilantro
1/2	teaspoon red pepper flakes

While steaks broil, mix salsa. In a small bowl, combine all ingredients. Serve each steak topped with this salsa.

VARIATION: Replace beef with fish, chicken, or pork. If you use pork, try apples in place of the pears.

*Try Jerk seasoning as a spice rub for meat, a way to perk up vegetables, a great omelet seasoner, a terrific way to jazz up sour cream on baked potatoes, and, of course, sprinkled into any salsa you wish.

My friend, Cynthia Rhine, never makes much mess when she whips up a meat loaf. Her secret? She mixes it with a pastry blender instead of getting her hands all mucky.

Muffin Cup Meat Loaves

1	pound ground sirloin
2	cups prepared frozen stuffing, thawed*
2	eggs
1/4	cup ketchup
2	tablespoons Worcestershire sauce
1/4	teaspoon sage
1/4	teaspoon dry mustard
1/4	teaspoon garlic salt
	Salt and pepper to taste

Preheat oven to 350 degrees F. In a large bowl, combine ground sirloin, stuffing, eggs, ketchup, Worcestershire sauce, and spices. Press mixture into 8 muffin tins and bake for 15 minutes. Quick chill, then freeze.

When ready to serve, thaw, then heat in microwave or regular oven at 350 degrees until warmed through and cooking is completed, another 5 minutes. Serves 2 per person.

VARIATION: Use 1 pound ground turkey instead of ground beef for a tasty dish with less fat.

*Stuffing is my secret ingredient for fabulous meat loaf. It already has everything in it—the onions, the bread, the seasonings—so it's super simple to throw together.

side dishes

Key Lime Pie Bread

1 3/4	cup sugar
2	eggs
1 3/4	cups all-purpose flour
1	teaspoon baking soda
1/2	teaspoon salt
1	cup applesauce
1/2	cup butter, melted
1/3	cup lime juice
1	package (8 ounces) cream cheese, softened

Preheat oven to 350 degrees F. Reserve 1/4 cup sugar and 1 egg for filling. In a large bowl, beat flour, 1 1/2 cup sugar, baking soda, salt, applesauce, 1 egg, butter, and lime juice until well mixed. Reserve 2 cups of batter. Pour remaining batter into greased and floured loaf pan.

Prepare filling: In a medium bowl, beat cream cheese with reserved 1/4 cup sugar and 1 egg. Drizzle over bread batter, swirling with knife. Cover with reserved batter and bake for 70 minutes. Cool 5 minutes, then remove from pan. Quick chill, then freeze.

When ready to serve, thaw at room temperature.

VARIATION: Use lemon or grapefruit juice in place of lime juice.

San Antonio Rice

4	cups cooked wild or white rice
1	can (15 ounces) black beans, drained
3	cups grated Monterey Jack cheese (or jalapeño Jack)
2	cups low-fat sour cream
1	can (5 ounces) mild green chilies, chopped
1	cup grated Cheddar cheese
	Salt and pepper to taste

In a large bowl, stir together rice, black beans, Jack cheese, sour cream, and chilies. Turn into buttered baking dish, and top with Cheddar cheese, salt, and pepper. Freeze.

When ready to serve, thaw and bake at 350 degrees F for 30 minutes.

VARIATION: You can turn this into a main course by adding 3 cups cooked, chopped chicken, beef, or seafood. Or for a spicier version, substitute chipotle or jalapeño chilies for mild green chilies.

TIP:
Keep cooked cauli-flower white with a sprinkling of lemon juice.

desserts

Chocolate Peanut Butter Pie

1	package (6 ounces) semisweet chocolate chips
3	tablespoons milk
2	tablespoons granulated sugar
4	eggs, separated
2	baked piecrusts, or 2 graham cracker crusts
1	cup peanut butter
1	package (8 ounces) cream cheese, softened
1	cup superfine sugar, or 1 cup granulated sugar whirled in food processor for 30 seconds
2	tablespoons butter, melted
1	cup whipping cream, whipped (makes 2 cups whipped)
1	tablespoon vanilla
1	cup frozen whipped topping, thawed, or 1 cup already whipped cream
	12 to 16 miniature chocolate peanut butter cups

In the top of a double boiler of simmering water, melt chocolate with milk and 2 tablespoons granulated sugar. Add egg yolks one at a time, stirring until well blended. Cool mixture.

In a small bowl, beat egg whites until stiff, but not dry. Fold into chocolate mixture, and pour half of mixture into each piecrust. Chill while you make the peanut butter layer.

In a large bowl, mix peanut butter, cream cheese, and superfine sugar until smooth. Add butter, two cups whipped cream, and vanilla. Mix well. Pour over chocolate layers and chill several hours.

Place a dollop of whipped cream on each intended slice, then nestle an unwrapped peanut butter cup in each dollop. You decide if you want to cut each pie into 6 or 8 slices! Wrap well and freeze.

TIP:

Before measuring peanut butter, honey, or other sticky ingredients, spray the measuring cup with nonstick coating.

Frozen Dessert Pops

To make these, use purchased plastic Popsicle molds or 8-ounce plastic cups with wooden sticks inserted in them. The shopping list includes ingredients for the first variation. Freeze for at least 3 hours.

Bavarian Strawberry Pops

3	cups fresh or frozen strawberries
1/4	cup sugar
1/2	cup water
1	package (3.4 ounces) instant vanilla pudding

Purée strawberries with sugar and water. Fill pop molds or cups half full. Freeze solid. While freezing, prepare instant vanilla pudding, following package directions. Top strawberry pops with pudding. Freeze again.

Chocolate–Peanut Butter Pops

1/2	cup water
1/4	cup sugar
1/4	cup creamy peanut butter
1	cup cream or milk
1	package (3.4 ounces) instant chocolate pudding

Boil water and sugar for 3 minutes. Remove from heat. Stir in peanut butter, then cream or milk. Fill Popsicle molds half full; freeze solid. Top with prepared instant chocolate pudding. Freeze again.

Banana Pops

1	banana, peeled
1	cup orange juice
	Magic Shell chocolate ice cream topping (optional)

Purée banana with orange juice. Fill Popsicle molds half full. Freeze. Dip each pop in Magic Shell chocolate ice cream topping for a hard, chocolatey coating.

Isn't it frustrating to cut cookies out from flattened dough, then have them smoosh or tear when you transfer them to the cookie sheet with a spatula? Next time, try this: Roll out the dough directly on the cookie sheet. Cut the shapes you want, then simply remove the parts in between.

Grape Pops

1	cup cream or milk
3/4	cup grape juice
1/4	cup sugar
1/4	cup lemon juice

Mix cream or milk with grape juice, sugar, and lemon juice. Fill Popsicle molds half full. Freeze.

VARIATION: Other fruit juices work well, too.

Piña Colada Pops

1	carton (8 ounces) vanilla yogurt
1	cup pineapple juice (reserved from crushed pineapple)
1/4	cup plus 1 teaspoon sugar
1	cup water
1	cup cream or milk
1/4	teaspoon coconut extract

Mix yogurt with pineapple juice and 1 teaspoon sugar. Fill Popsicle molds half full. Freeze solid. Boil water and 1/4 cup sugar for 3 minutes. Remove from heat. Stir in cream or milk and coconut extract. Pour into pop molds over pineapple layer. Freeze again.

week four

Main Dishes

Aunt Beulah's Ham and Corn Soup

Ham and Creamy Mustard Melts

Honey Roasted Ham

Pizza Bread Roll

Too-Good-for-Most-Company Shrimp Jambalaya

Side Dishes

Fresh Garden Casserole

Cheesy Corn Casserole

Desserts

Ice Cream Sandwiches

Vermont Maple Tree Pumpkin Cheesecake

shopping list

The following list is exactly what you'll need for the week's dinners, so shop accordingly. You need only purchase those items you don't already have on hand.

BAKING MIXES AND FLOURS

1 package (8.5 ounces) corn muffin mix

BREADS AND GRAINS/PASTA/RICE

1 loaf frozen bread dough
1 1/2 cups graham cracker crumbs
4 sesame hoagie sandwich rolls
1 1/2 cups uncooked wild rice

CHEESE/DAIRY/EGGS

1 cup grated Cheddar cheese
4 packages (8 ounces each) cream cheese, regular or reduced fat
2 pounds grated Monterey Jack or Swiss cheese
2 cups grated jalapeño Monterey Jack cheese (or regular Jack)
1/2 pound grated mozzarella cheese
1/4 cup freshly grated Parmesan cheese
1/2 cup plus 1/3 cup butter
1/4 cup heavy cream
1 cup half-and-half
1/4 gallon caramel fudge ice cream
3 cups milk
3 1/2 cups sour cream (low-fat works well, too)
5 eggs

CONDIMENTS AND SAUCES

1/4 cup whole-grain mustard
2 kosher dill pickles (optional, for ham melts)
1 cup bottled pizza sauce
8 drops Tabasco sauce

12 tablespoon-cubes frozen white sauce (or 6 tablespoons each butter and flour)

FLAVORINGS/HERBS*/ SEASONINGS/SPICES

1 tablespoon chopped fresh basil
1 bay leaf
1 1/2 teaspoons cinnamon
1 teaspoon ground cloves
1 1/2 teaspoons ground ginger
1/2 teaspoon nutmeg
Salt and pepper
1/2 teaspoon red (cayenne) pepper
1/4 teaspoon white pepper

FRUITS/NUTS/VEGETABLES

1/4 cup sliced almonds
1/3 cup ground almonds or pecans
1 cup nuts (optional, for ice cream sandwiches)
1 cup crushed pecans (optional, for ice cream sandwiches)
1 cup frozen chopped asparagus (or use fresh)
1 cup green or lima beans, fresh or frozen
2 cups frozen broccoli florets
1 cup frozen sliced carrots or baby carrots
1 package (16 ounces) plus 2 1/2 cups frozen corn
1 can (16 ounces) creamed corn
2 teaspoons minced garlic
1/2 cup sliced mushrooms (optional, for pizza bread roll)
1 cup frozen okra
4 cups fresh or frozen chopped onion

1 green bell pepper (optional, for pizza bread roll)
1 cup solid pack canned pumpkin
1 can (16 ounces) tomatoes
1 can (6 ounces) sliced water chestnuts

LIQUIDS

2 cups (or 1 1/2 cans) fish or chicken stock, or chicken broth
3 cups vegetable stock or chicken stock, or 2 1/2 cans broth

MEAT/SEAFOOD

9 1/2 pounds precooked ham
1/2 pound oysters or mixed seafood (crawfish, mussels, scallops, crab, your choice)
1 pound shrimp, fresh or frozen
1/2 pound smoked sausage

OILS

4 tablespoons olive or vegetable oil
Olive oil or vegetable oil spray

SWEETS AND SWEETENERS

1 package (12 ounces) semisweet chocolate chips
16 ounces white chocolate or semisweet chocolate bar
1 cup honey
5 tablespoons maple syrup
1 can (6 ounces) frozen orange juice concentrate
2 cups plus 1 tablespoon brown sugar
1 1/2 cups granulated sugar

*If using fresh herbs, double the amount listed here.

PUTTING IT ALL TOGETHER

1. Thaw 12 tablespoon-cubes of frozen white sauce mix, or mix 6 tablespoons each of flour and butter into a paste.

3. Grate cheese (if not already grated).

2. Thaw onions, any frozen vegetables, frozen orange juice, and bread dough. Soften ice cream and cream cheese.

3. In a large skillet, sauté onions in 2 tablespoons vegetable oil.

4. Melt chocolate for ice cream sandwiches. Make the ice cream sandwiches.

5. From the cooked ham, chop 3/4 pound, thinly slice 1 pound, dice 2 cups, and leave 6 pounds intact for Honey Roasted Ham recipe.

6. Rinse and shell or peel seafood. Slice sausage.

7. Butter two 9 × 13-inch casserole dishes and a square or 10-inch-round baking dish.

8. Toast almonds in a dry skillet over medium heat, stirring for 1 to 2 minutes.

from pantry to plate

Using everything you have just prepared, create these simple, tasty dishes.

main dishes

Aunt Beulah's Ham and Corn Soup

4	tablespoon-cubes white sauce, thawed (or 2 tablespoons each butter and flour, combined)
1	cup milk
1	cup half-and-half
3	cups vegetable or chicken stock or 2 1/2 cans broth
1	tablespoon brown sugar
1/4	teaspoon white pepper
2	cups diced cooked ham
1	package (16 ounces) frozen corn, thawed
1/2	cup sautéed chopped onion

In a large soup pot, melt white sauce cubes or butter and flour over low heat. Stir in milk and half-and-half until sauce thickens. Stir in stock, brown sugar, and white pepper. Add ham, corn, and onion. Heat through, but do not boil. Quick chill, then freeze.

When ready to serve, heat in top of double boiler over simmering water until heated through, 5 to 10 minutes.

VARIATION: Use white lima beans instead of corn.

Ham and Creamy Mustard Melts

Olive oil or vegetable oil spray
1/2   cup sour cream
1/4   cup whole-grain mustard
4   sesame hoagie sandwich rolls, split
1   pound cooked ham, thinly sliced
2   kosher dill pickles, sliced (optional)
2   pounds grated Monterey Jack or Swiss cheese

Spray griddle with oil. In a small bowl, whisk together sour cream and mustard until well blended. Spread on all cut sides of rolls. Place bottom halves of rolls on griddle, cut sides up. Top with ham and, if desired, dill pickles.

Being careful not to touch griddle, mound a generous handful of cheese atop each sandwich, allowing the cheese to melt and fry as it falls down sides of bun. Just as cheese in center melts, cover with top roll half, pressing down so bread will adhere to cheese. Remove entire sandwich with spatula. Quick cool and freeze, wrapping tightly in foil.

When ready to serve, bake at 350 degrees F for 15 minutes, or until cheese is bubbly again.

Serving Suggestion: *Serve with Fresh Garden Casserole* (see page 105).

Honey Roasted Ham

1	cup honey
1	can (6 ounces) frozen orange juice concentrate, thawed
1	teaspoon ground cloves
6	pounds cooked ham
2	cups brown sugar

Preheat oven to 400 degrees F. In a small microwave-safe bowl, heat honey with juice concentrate and cloves in microwave until honey stirs easily, about a minute. Mix well and spread over ham in roasting pan. Press brown sugar onto honey mixture, encasing ham in this "crust." Bake for 15 minutes. Freeze.

Before serving, thaw in refrigerator a day and a half. Bring to room temperature, or cover with foil and heat at 300 degrees F for 30 minutes.

Serving Suggestion: Serve warm with buttery brussels sprouts and *Cheesy Corn Casserole (see page 106).*

A newlywed husband noticed that his wife always cut off the end of the ham before she cooked it. When he asked why, she explained that her mother always did it that way. When he asked his mother-in-law why she always cut the end off of the ham, she said, "Grandma always did it that way." Finally, he asked Grandma, who shrugged and said, "I always cut the end off my hams because my pan was too short."

Pizza Bread Roll

	Vegetable oil spray
1	frozen bread dough loaf, thawed
1	cup bottled pizza sauce
1/4	pound chopped ham
1/2	pound grated mozzarella cheese
1/4	cup freshly grated Parmesan cheese
1/2	cup sliced mushrooms
1	green bell pepper, chopped,
1	small onion, chopped
	Other pizza toppings of your choice (optional)
1	egg, beaten

Preheat oven to 400 degrees F. Spray baking sheet with oil. On a floured surface, roll loaf into rectangle, about 12 × 16 inches. Spread with pizza sauce. Sprinkle with ham, cheeses, and toppings, if desired. Roll tightly, beginning at short end, and place seam-down on baking sheet. Brush with beaten egg. Cut four slits in dough to vent. Bake 25 minutes. Quick cool and freeze.

When ready to serve, thaw overnight in refrigerator, heat in oven, covered, at 300 degrees F for 10 minutes. Slice and serve.

VARIATION: Use cooked sausage or pepperoni instead of ham.

NOTE: This makes an easy take-along lunch, too. Double the recipe and keep a pizza roll frozen for later.

TIP:

Use a pizza cutter for cutting and slicing instead of a knife. It's the better choice in many cases.

Too-Good-for-Most-Company Shrimp Jambalaya

1	pound shrimp
1/2	pound oysters or other seafood (crawfish, mussels, scallops, crab)
1/2	pound smoked sausage, sliced
1/2	pound chopped cooked ham (or pork or chicken)
2	cups fish or chicken stock (or broth)
1 1/2	cups uncooked wild rice
1	can (16 ounces) tomatoes
1/2	cup sautéed chopped onion
1	cup frozen okra, thawed
1	tablespoon chopped fresh basil
2	teaspoons minced garlic
1/2	teaspoon red (cayenne) pepper
1	bay leaf
	Salt and pepper to taste

Preheat oven to 350 degrees F. Place all ingredients in a buttered 9 × 13-inch baking dish or casserole. Cover tightly and cook for 1 hour. Quick chill, then freeze.

When ready to serve, bake casserole at 350 degrees F for 30 minutes.

VARIATIONS: Stir in a cup each of sautéed celery and green onions when serving. Or, instead of baking the jambalaya in a standard oven, reduce your cooking time by using the microwave: Cook jambalaya in a covered microwave-safe casserole dish for 10 minutes on high, then 15 minutes at the 50 percent power setting.

side dishes

Fresh Garden Casserole

2	tablespoons olive or vegetable oil
2	cups frozen broccoli florets, thawed
1	cup frozen sliced carrots or baby carrots, thawed
1	cup sautéed chopped onion
1	cup chopped asparagus, fresh or frozen and thawed
1	cup frozen corn, thawed
1	cup green or lima beans, fresh or frozen and thawed
1	can (6 ounces) sliced water chestnuts, drained
8	tablespoon-cubes frozen white sauce (or 4 tablespoons each butter and flour, combined)
2	cups milk
8	drops Tabasco sauce
1	cup grated Cheddar cheese

In a skillet over medium heat, cook vegetables in oil until almost tender. Place vegetables in buttered 9 × 13-inch casserole. Wipe out skillet with paper towel. Reduce heat to low, and return skillet to heat. Melt white sauce cubes or flour and butter in skillet, stirring until smooth. Add milk and Tabasco, stirring to form creamy sauce. Stir in cheese just until melted. Pour over vegetables, quick cool, and freeze.

When ready to serve, thaw and bake, at 350 degrees F for 25 minutes, or until hot.

VARIATION: This casserole is so versatile; substitute other veggies, or add 4 cups cooked pasta to make it a vegetarian main dish. Another idea, if you love potatoes, is to add cooked, cubed potatoes when you reheat it. (Remember, potatoes don't freeze well unless mashed.)

Cheesy Corn Casserole

1	can (16 ounces) creamed corn
1 1/2	cups frozen corn, slightly thawed
2	cups grated jalapeño Monterey Jack cheese
1/2	cup butter, melted
1	cup low-fat sour cream
1	package (8.5 ounces) corn muffin mix

Preheat oven to 350 degrees F. In a large bowl, combine all ingredients. Pour into buttered square or 10-inch-round baking dish and bake 1 hour. Quick cool and freeze.

When ready to serve, thaw at room temperature and heat, wrapped in foil, in an oven at 300 degrees F for 30 minutes.

VARIATION: Use regular Jack cheese for a milder version.

NOTE: This recipe doubles well if you want to freeze two casseroles, or if you want to serve a crowd.

desserts

Ice Cream Sandwiches

1/4	gallon caramel fudge ice cream, softened
16	Chocolate Chunk Cookies *(see page 231)*
1	package (12 ounces) semisweet chocolate chips
1	cup crushed pecans or other nuts (optional)

Spread softened ice cream between two cookies, forming a sandwich. Freeze. Melt chocolate chips in top of double boiler over simmering water. Hand dip ice cream sandwiches into melted chocolate, then, if desired, into crushed nuts. Freeze. When set, wrap each sandwich tightly in plastic and return to freezer.

NOTE: For best results, prepare ice cream sandwiches at least a day ahead of time, so the cookies will have time to soften by absorbing moisture from the ice cream.

Vermont Maple Tree Pumpkin Cheesecake

Crust

1 1/2	cups graham cracker crumbs
1/3	cup ground almonds or pecans
1/2	teaspoon ground ginger
1/2	teaspoon cinnamon
1/3	cup butter, melted

Filling

4	packages (8 ounces each) cream cheese, softened
1 1/4	cups granulated sugar
3	tablespoons maple syrup
1	teaspoon ground ginger
1	teaspoon cinnamon
1/2	teaspoon nutmeg
4	eggs at room temperature
1/4	cup heavy cream
1	cup solid pack canned pumpkin

Topping

2	cups sour cream
1/4	cup granulated sugar
2	tablespoons maple syrup
1/4	cup toasted sliced almonds

Preheat oven to 425 degrees F. In a medium bowl, mix crust ingredients together and press onto bottom of a 10-inch springform pan. Bake 10 minutes. Remove and reduce oven temperature to 325 degrees F.

In a large bowl, beat cream cheese until smooth. Add sugar, syrup, ginger, cinnamon, and nutmeg. Blend thoroughly. Add eggs one at a time, beating after each. Add cream and pumpkin. Mix well. Pour into crust. Bake 45 minutes. Turn off oven, and don't open oven door for 1 hour. Remove cheesecake.

To make topping, preheat oven to 425 degrees F. Beat sour cream, sugar, and syrup. Pour over cheesecake and bake 10 minutes. Cool to room temperature (about an hour), then arrange almonds on topping. Freeze.

When ready to serve, thaw to room temperature. Cheesecakes taste best with the chill off, so don't serve it too cold.

Friday

TIP:
Need another cooling rack? Invert a muffin tin.

week five

Menu

Main Dishes

Cheesehead Chipotle Frittata

Chicken Papaya Quesadillas

Macadamia-Crusted Chicken with Ginger Aioli

Mexican Chicken Lasagna

Pesto Pepper Chicken Pizza

Desserts

Carrot Cake

Designer Cookies

shopping list

The following list is exactly what you'll need for the week's dinners, so shop accordingly. You need only purchase those items you don't already have on hand.

BAKING MIXES AND FLOURS

3 1/2 teaspoons baking soda
6 1/2 cups all-purpose flour

BREADS AND GRAINS/PASTA/RICE

2 cups cornbread
1 store-bought pizza crust
10 (10-inch) flour tortillas

CHEESE/DAIRY/EGGS

4 1/3 cups grated Cheddar cheese
1 package (8 ounces) cream cheese
4 to 5 cups grated low-fat Monterey Jack cheese
2 cups grated mozzarella cheese
1/3 cup freshly grated Parmesan or Romano cheese
24 tablespoons (3 sticks) butter
1 1/4 cups buttermilk
2 cups sour cream
13 eggs

CONDIMENTS AND SAUCES

1 cup mayonnaise
1 teaspoon whole-grain mustard

1 cup bottled pesto sauce
2 cups store-bought salsa

FLAVORINGS/HERBS*/ SEASONINGS/SPICES

1/2 cup minced cilantro
2 teaspoons cinnamon
3 tablespoons chopped Italian parsley
Salt and pepper
5 teaspoons vanilla

FRUITS/NUTS/VEGETABLES

Juice of 1 lemon
1 teaspoon orange juice
1 teaspoon orange zest
2 papayas
1 can (8 ounces) crushed pineapple
3 1/3 ounces shredded coconut
2 cups macadamia nuts
1/2 cup pine nuts
1 cup chopped walnuts or pecans (optional, for Carrot Cake)
2 avocados
3 carrots, grated (2 cups)
3 cans (5 ounces each) chopped mild green or chipotle chilies

1 can (5 ounces) chopped chipotle chilies in adobo sauce
1 teaspoon minced garlic
1 teaspoon grated fresh ginger
2 cups sliced mushrooms
1 can (4.5 ounces) chopped black olives
1 can (4.5 ounces) sliced black olives
7 cups fresh or frozen chopped onion
2 cups bottled roasted red peppers

MEAT/SEAFOOD

13 boneless, skinless split chicken breasts

OILS

4 tablespoons olive oil
1 1/2 cups shortening
3/4 cup vegetable oil

SWEETS AND SWEETENERS

1 tablespoon corn syrup
1 cup brown sugar
4 cups granulated sugar
2 cups powdered sugar

*If using fresh herbs, double the amount listed here.

PUTTING IT ALL TOGETHER

1. Thaw onions. Soften butter and cream cheese.

2. In medium skillet over medium heat, sauté chopped onion in 4 tablespoons olive oil for 7 to 8 minutes, or until transparent to yield 3 1/2 cups sautéed onion.

3. In a large pot of simmering water, cook 9 chicken breasts until no longer pink. Drain and cool.

4. Peel, seed, and slice the papayas.

5. Crumble bread crumbs by hand, or whirl in blender.

6. Set aside 4 split chicken breasts for Macadamia-Crusted Chicken.

7. Grate carrots. Grate cheese (if not already grated). Slice mushrooms.

8. Rinse and chop cilantro and parsley.

9. Grease one 9 × 13-inch baking pan, two loaf pans, and two round 9-inch cake pans or one 9 × 13-inch baking pan.

10. Chop bottled red peppers.

Using everything you have just prepared, create the following simple, tasty dishes.

main dishes

Cheesehead Chipotle Frittata

2	tablespoons olive oil or melted butter
1/2	cup sautéed chopped onion
2	cups sliced mushrooms
1	cup bottled roasted red peppers, chopped
1	can (5 ounces) chopped chipotle chilies in adobo sauce
6	eggs
1/3	cup grated Parmesan or Romano cheese
1/3	cup grated Cheddar cheese
3	tablespoons chopped Italian parsley
	Salt and pepper to taste

Place oil, onion, mushrooms, peppers, and chilies in a large, ovenproof skillet. In a medium bowl, whip eggs with cheeses, parsley, salt, and pepper. Pour over vegetables. Cook over medium heat without stirring, until edges begin to tan. Dust with additional Parmesan cheese if desired, and place under broiler until lightly browned (just a minute or two). Quick cool, then freeze.

When ready to serve, thaw and enjoy at room temperature, or heat it wrapped in foil at 350 degrees F for 20 minutes. Slice into wedges.

VARIATIONS: Make a milder version using chopped mild green chilies.

Serving Suggestion: Focaccia bread and seasonal fruit make good accompaniments.

These Italian omelets are so versatile; they make a hearty dinner, a super breakfast, a delicious tailgate meal (they're good hot or cold), even a great appetizer if cut into small pieces. This one is vegetarian, but you can always add a cup of cooked seafood, pork, or chicken. Again, experiment with the ingredients—swap green bell peppers for roasted red ones, garlic instead of parsley. Try spinach or artichokes instead of mushrooms, or sautéed green onions in place of white ones. Just remember that green onions don't freeze well.

Tuesday

Chicken Papaya Quesadillas

My friend, Christy Noll, showed me the easiest way to dice an avocado. First, cut the avocado in half and remove the pit (whack the pit with a sharp knife, then pull it out). Then using a dull knife, hold the avocado—peel side down—right in your hand, and slice the flesh as it sits in the peel. A dull knife will ensure that you won't pierce the skin and cut yourself. Slice one way, then criss-cross the other way. Turn the avocado upside down, invert the peel, and the cubes will fall off. (You can also cube a fresh mango this way.)

6	(10-inch) flour tortillas
4	skinless, boneless chicken half-breasts, cooked and shredded
2	papayas, peeled, seeded, and sliced
2	cups sautéed chopped onion
2	cans (5 ounces each) chopped mild green or chipotle chilies
1/2	cup minced cilantro
	Salt and pepper to taste
4 to 5	cups grated low-fat Monterey Jack cheese
1	cup sour cream
1	cup store-bought salsa
2	avocados, peeled, pitted, and sliced

Preheat oven to 425 degrees F. Place 3 tortillas on a baking sheet. Top with chicken, papaya slices, onion, chilies, cilantro, salt, and pepper, then cheese. Press another tortilla onto each cheese-covered tortilla. Bake for 8 minutes, or until cheese melts. Quick chill, then freeze.

When ready to serve, bake at 350 degrees F for 12 minutes. Cut each quesadilla into quarters, and serve three slices per person. Don't forget to top the quesadillas with dollops of sour cream, salsa, and slices of avocado.

VARIATION: Try avocado or roasted red peppers in place of the papaya, if you wish. If you prefer a spicier version, use jalapeño Jack cheese.

Serving Suggestion: A fresh green salad makes a nice side dish.

Macadamia-Crusted Chicken with Ginger Aioli

4	boneless, skinless split chicken breasts
	Salt and pepper
1/2	cup all-purpose flour
2	eggs, beaten
2	cups macadamia nuts, finely ground*
2	tablespoons olive oil

Preheat oven to 350 degrees F. Sprinkle chicken with salt and pepper, then coat with flour, dip into eggs, and coat with ground nuts.

Heat oil in a large skillet over medium heat. Cook breasts in oil just until golden brown, about 4 minutes per side. Place in baking dish. Bake for 30 minutes. Quick cool and freeze.

When ready to serve, thaw in refrigerator and warm at 300 degrees F, wrapped in foil to retain moistness, for about 15 minutes. Prepare Ginger Aioli (do not freeze aioli).

Ginger Aioli

1	cup mayonnaise
	Juice of 1 lemon
1	teaspoon whole-grain mustard
1	teaspoon grated fresh ginger

Combine all ingredients in a small bowl. Serve a dollop of Ginger Aioli on each piece of Macadamia-Crusted Chicken.

TIP:

You'll get more juice from a lemon if you heat it first in the microwave. You can also roll it on the countertop, pressing down as it rolls, to break up the membranes inside and release more juice.

*Chop nuts in blender or food processor fitted with metal blade until finely ground.

Mexican Chicken Lasagna

4   boneless, skinless chicken half-breasts, cooked and shredded

1   cup bottled salsa

1   can (5 ounces) chopped mild green or chipotle chilies

1   teaspoon minced garlic

1   can (4.5 ounces) chopped black olives

1   cup sour cream

4   (10-inch) flour tortillas, cut into 2-inch strips

2   cups cornbread crumbs

4   cups grated Cheddar cheese

Preheat oven to 350 degrees F. In a large bowl, mix chicken, salsa, chilies, garlic, olives, and sour cream. Place half the tortilla strips in the bottom of a greased 9 × 13-inch baking dish. Pour half the chicken mixture onto the tortilla strips. Sprinkle with half the cornbread crumbs, then half the cheese. Repeat layers. Bake for 15 minutes. Quick cool, then freeze.

When ready to serve, bake at 350 degrees F for 25 minutes.

VARIATION: This is an easy and delicious recipe, but if you prefer a layered appearance, take a little more time and layer—rather than mix—the sour cream and salsa.

NOTE: Let the kids make this streamlined recipe while you put your feet up! To make it even easier, use canned chicken.

Pesto Pepper Chicken Pizza

1	cup bottled pesto sauce
1	store-bought pizza crust
1	cup bottled roasted red peppers, sliced
3	cups shredded cooked chicken
1	cup sautéed chopped onion
1	can (4.5 ounces) sliced black olives
1/2	cup pine nuts
2	cups grated mozzarella cheese

If you like homemade pesto, consider using cilantro or other herbs in place of the basil.

Preheat oven to 400 degrees F. Spread pesto over pizza crust. Top with remaining ingredients, and bake for 10 to 15 minutes, or until cheese is bubbly. Quick cool, then freeze.

When ready to serve, wrap in foil and bake at 350 degrees F for 20 minutes, or until bubbly. Slice into 6 wedges.

VARIATION: Our kids often bring friends for dinner, so the way I make most pizzas is to buy two pizza crust mixes, prepare as directed, then press the dough into a jelly roll pan. I double the toppings, and bake. Then we cut the pizza into squares.

desserts

Carrot Cake

2	cups all-purpose flour
2	teaspoons baking soda
2	teaspoons cinnamon
1/2	teaspoon salt
3	eggs
3/4	cup vegetable oil
3/4	cup buttermilk
2	cups sugar
2	teaspoons vanilla
1	can (8 ounces) crushed pineapple, drained
2	cups grated carrots
3 1/3	ounces shredded coconut
1	cup chopped walnuts or pecans (optional)
	Buttermilk Glaze *(recipe follows)*
	Cream Cheese Frosting *(recipe follows)*

Preheat oven to 350 degrees F. Sift flour, soda, cinnamon, and salt into a medium bowl. In a large bowl, beat eggs, oil, buttermilk, sugar, and vanilla. Add flour mixture, pineapple, carrots, coconut, and, if desired, nuts. Stir well. Pour into 2 greased 9-inch cake pans and bake for 30 to 35 minutes, or a 9 × 13-inch baking pan and bake for 55 minutes. Cake is done when toothpick tests clean.

While cake bakes, prepare glaze. When cake is finished, pour glaze over hot cake. Cool 15 minutes, so glaze can soak in. Freeze.

When ready to serve, thaw at room temperature, then ice with Cream Cheese Frosting.

TIP:

For moister cakes, always cook them 25 degrees cooler than called for, and 5 minutes less.

Buttermilk Glaze

1	cup sugar
1/2	teaspoon baking soda
1/2	cup buttermilk
8	tablespoons (1 stick) butter
1	tablespoon corn syrup
1	teaspoon vanilla

Combine all ingredients except vanilla in a small saucepan over medium-high heat. Boil for 5 minutes, stirring occasionally. Remove from heat and stir in vanilla. Pour over cake.

Cream Cheese Frosting

8	tablespoons (1 stick) butter
1	package (8 ounces) cream cheese, softened
1	teaspoon vanilla
2	cups powdered sugar
1	teaspoon orange juice
1	teaspoon orange zest

In a large bowl, cream butter and cheese until fluffy. Add remaining ingredients and mix until smooth. Frost thawed Carrot Cake.

TIP:

If a recipe calls for a cup of buttermilk you can make a substitute by mixing a tablespoon of lemon juice or vinegar with enough milk to equal a cup.

Designer Cookies

1 1/2	cups shortening
8	tablespoons (1 stick) butter, softened
1	cup granulated sugar
1	cup brown sugar
2	eggs
1	teaspoon vanilla
4	cups sifted all-purpose flour
1	teaspoon baking soda
1/2	teaspoon salt

In a large bowl, beat shortening, butter, and sugars until well mixed. Beat in eggs and vanilla. Sift in flour, soda, and salt. Stir. Divide dough into 5 portions, flavoring each one differently if you wish. Shape into rolls, wrap, and freeze.

To bake, preheat oven to 375 degrees F. Cut frozen dough into 1/4-inch slices and bake 2 inches apart on an ungreased baking sheet for about 10 minutes. Each batch will yield about 3 dozen cookies.

VARIATIONS:

1. The ever-popular Chocolate Chip Cookies: Simply stir in 6 ounces of chocolate chips.
2. Hazelnut Cookies: Stir in 1/2 cup of crushed hazelnuts.
3. Strawberry Tarts: Substitute strawberry extract for vanilla, then spoon a dab of strawberry jam on half the slices. Cut a hole in the center of the remaining slices, place over bottom slices, and pinch edges to seal.
4. Peanut Butter Cookies: Substitute 1/2 cup peanut butter for 1/2 cup butter.
5. Spice Cookies: Add 1/2 teaspoon each cinnamon, cloves, and ginger.
6. Coconut-Macadamia Cookies: Add 1/2 cup flaked coconut and 1/2 cup crushed macadamia nuts.
7. Candy Bar Cookies: Add your favorite candy bar, crushed.
8. Key Lime Cookies: Add 1 tablespoon of grated lime rind and 6 drops of green food coloring.
9. Peppermint Crunch Christmas Cookies: Add 1/2 cup finely crushed candy canes.

The Once-a-Week Cookbook

week six

Menu

Main Dishes

Elena's Tortilla Soup

Cattle Boys' Beef Onion Stew

Pizza in a Pot

Spicy Steaks with Honey-Mustard Sauce

Warm Up the Winter Beefy Pot Pie

Desserts

Barbara Murphy's Fresh Apple Cake

Chocolate Macadamia Pie

shopping list

The following list is exactly what you'll need for the week's dinners, so shop accordingly.
You need only purchase those items you don't already have on hand.

BAKING MIXES AND FLOURS

1 teaspoon baking soda
3 1/2 cups all-purpose flour

BREADS AND GRAINS/PASTA/RICE

3 (9-inch) uncooked piecrusts
1 package (6.75 ounces) tortilla chips
1/2 pound pasta (fusilli, shell, elbow, wagon wheel, your choice)

CHEESE/DAIRY/EGGS

1/2 pound Cheddar cheese, grated
1/4 pound Monterey Jack cheese, grated
1/2 cup freshly grated Parmesan cheese
3 tablespoons butter
2 tablespoons sour cream
Whipped cream (optional, for pie)
5 eggs

CONDIMENTS AND SAUCES

1/4 cup whole-grain mustard
2 cans or jars (16 ounces each) tomato salsa
1/2 cup tomato paste
8 tablespoon-cubes frozen white sauce (or 4 tablespoons each butter and flour)

FLAVORINGS/HERBS*/ SEASONINGS/SPICES

3 tablespoons chili powder
1/2 teaspoon cinnamon
3 teaspoons ground cumin
1 teaspoon curry powder
3 teaspoons garlic powder
3 tablespoons oregano
1 1/8 teaspoons red (cayenne) pepper
1 tablespoon fresh minced rosemary, or 1 teaspoon dried
Salt and pepper
1/4 teaspoon dried thyme, or 1/2 teaspoon fresh
3 teaspoons vanilla

FRUITS/NUTS/VEGETABLES

6 apples, or enough to make 3 cups chopped
1 tablespoon lime juice
3/4 cup macadamia nuts
1 cup chopped walnuts or pecans (optional, for cake)
2 cups frozen sliced carrots
2 cans (5 ounces each) chopped mild green or chipotle chilies
3 teaspoons crushed garlic
1/2 cup sliced mushrooms, fresh or canned
1 can (5 ounces) sliced mushrooms
1/2 cup sliced olives
7 cups fresh or frozen chopped onion

1 package (10 ounces) frozen peas
1 package (10 ounces) frozen carrots
1 red or green bell pepper
1 can (15 ounces) stewed tomatoes, Italian style

LIQUIDS

9 cups or 6 cans (14.5 ounces each) beef stock or broth

MEAT/SEAFOOD

13 boneless beef rib eye or top loin steaks, cut 1-inch thick
2 pounds flank steak or rib eye steak, for stew

OILS

3 tablespoons cooking oil
2 tablespoons olive oil
1 cup and 3 tablespoons vegetable oil

SWEETS AND SWEETENERS

3/4 cup chocolate chips
Chocolate shavings (optional, for pie)
1/2 cup cocoa
1/2 cup corn syrup
1/3 cup honey
3 cups sugar
Powdered sugar for dusting cake

*If using fresh herbs, double the amount listed here.

PUTTING IT ALL TOGETHER

1. Thaw 8 tablespoon-cubes frozen white sauce mix, or mix 4 tablespoons each flour and butter. Thaw piecrusts.

2. Thaw frozen vegetables. In a large skillet, sauté chopped onions in 3 tablespoons cooking oil until transparent.

3. Chop bell pepper. Chop mushrooms if necessary.

4. Bake 1 pie shell according to package directions. Bring other 2 to room temperature and roll together, on a floured surface, into a 9 × 13-inch rectangle.

5. In a small bowl, combine 3 teaspoons each chili powder, cumin, garlic powder, oregano, and 1 teaspoon red pepper to make the spice rub for Spicy Steaks with Honey-Mustard Sauce. Reserve one-third of it in your pantry for Cha-Cha Chicken in Week Eleven *(see chapter 17, page 190)*.

6. Rub the other two-thirds of the spice rub on both sides of 8 rib eye steaks. Prepare Spicy Steaks with Honey-Mustard Sauce. Remove 4 of the cooked steaks and dice, reserving for Elena's Tortilla Soup. Cook the remaining 5 steaks separately until rare; then cube them.

7. Sauté 2 pounds of flank steak or rib eyes (for stew) in 3 tablespoons vegetable oil.

8. Grease and flour a Bundt pan.

Using everything you have just prepared, create these simple, tasty dishes.

Main Dishes

Elena's Tortilla Soup

4	cooked and diced seasoned steaks
4	cups beef stock or broth
1	can or jar (16 ounces) tomato salsa
1	cup sautéed chopped onion
1	can (5 ounces) chopped mild green or chipotle chilies
1	package (6.75 ounces) tortilla chips
1	cup grated Cheddar cheese

Combine diced steaks with broth, salsa, onion, and chilies in a freezer container. Freeze.

When ready to serve, warm in large soup pot over low heat until heated through. Break chips into soup and stir in Cheddar cheese. Serve hot.

VARIATION: If you want to make it Central American style, substitute jalapeños for the mild green chilies.

Cattle Boys' Beef Onion Stew

2	pounds cooked beef (rib eye or flank steak), cubed
1	cup sautéed chopped onion
2	cups frozen sliced carrots, thawed
1	can or jar (16 ounces) tomato salsa
1	can (5 ounces) chopped mild green or chipotle chilies
1	can (5 ounces) sliced mushrooms
4	tablespoon-cubes white sauce, thawed (or 2 tablespoons each flour and butter mixed together)
1	tablespoon oregano
1	teaspoon crushed garlic
1/2	teaspoon ground black pepper
2	cups beef stock or broth

Place all ingredients except broth in freezer container; mix well. Freeze.

When ready to serve, heat with broth in a large soup pot over medium heat, stirring until carrots soften, sauce cubes or flour and butter melt, and sauce thickens.

Serving Suggestion: Serve over fluffy white rice. Biscuits or hot rolls round out this hearty meal.

TIP:
Potato flakes are great for thickening too-thin sauces and soups.

Pizza in a Pot

2	cups beef stock or broth
1	can (15 ounces) stewed tomatoes, Italian style
1	cup sautéed chopped onion
1	red or green bell pepper, chopped
1/2	cup sliced mushrooms
1/2	cup sliced olives
1/2	cup tomato paste
2 to 3	teaspoons oregano
1	teaspoon crushed garlic
1/2	teaspoon ground black pepper
1/2	pound dry pasta (fusilli, wagon wheel, shell, elbow macaroni, your choice)
3	boneless beef top loin or rib eye steaks, cooked rare and cubed
1	cup grated Cheddar cheese
1	cup grated Monterey Jack cheese
1/2	cup freshly grated Parmesan cheese

In a large soup pot, bring beef stock to boil. Add tomatoes, onion, bell pepper, mushrooms, olives, tomato paste, oregano, garlic, and black pepper. Simmer for 30 minutes. Stir in pasta and cook *al dente,* about 10 more minutes. You may need to add more liquid.

Preheat oven to 350 degrees F. Stir beef into stock and vegetable mixture. Pour one-third into 10-inch square or round casserole dish. Follow with one-third of the cheeses, then repeat layers twice. Bake 20 minutes or until cheese is bubbly. Quick cool, then freeze.

When ready to serve, bake frozen casserole at 350 degrees F for 20 minutes.

The Once-a-Week Cookbook

Spicy Steaks with Honey-Mustard Sauce

2	tablespoons olive oil
4	boneless beef top loin or rib eye steaks, cut 1-inch thick and seasoned with spice rub

Heat oil in a large skillet over medium heat. Place steaks in skillet for 10 to 12 minutes, turning once. If serving steaks immediately, prepare Honey-Mustard Sauce.

If freezing, quick cool steaks, wrap, and freeze. Prepare and freeze sauce separately, or prepare sauce when you reheat the steaks. Warm thawed steaks at 300 degrees F for 10 minutes, taking care not to over-cook the meat. Warm sauce before drizzling over steaks.

Serving Suggestion: Try Chocolate Macadamia Pie (page 134) for dessert.

Honey-Mustard Sauce

1/3	cup honey
1/4	cup whole-grain mustard
2	tablespoons sour cream
1	tablespoon lime juice
1	tablespoon fresh minced rosemary, or 1 teaspoon dried

Mix honey, mustard, sour cream, lime juice, and rosemary in a small saucepan over medium heat, stirring just until bubbly. Serve hot, over steaks.

Warm Up the Winter Beefy Pot Pie

1	package (10 ounces) frozen peas and carrots, thawed
1/2	cup sautéed chopped onion
1	cup beef stock or broth
4	tablespoon-cubes frozen white sauce, thawed (or 2 table-spoons each flour and butter mixed together)
1	teaspoon crushed garlic
1/2	teaspoon ground black pepper
1/4	teaspoon dried thyme, or 1/2 teaspoon fresh
2	boneless beef top loin or rib eye steaks, cooked rare and cubed
2	piecrusts formed into 9 × 13-inch rectangles

Preheat oven to 400 degrees F. In a large skillet, stir peas, carrots, onion, stock, white sauce cubes or flour and butter, garlic, pepper, and thyme until sauce thickens. Stir in beef. Pour mixture into 9 × 13-inch baking dish. Place piecrust rectangle atop beef mixture.* Vent crust by piercing several times with a fork. Bake for 20 minutes, or until crust is golden. Quick cool, then freeze.

When ready to serve, bake frozen dish at 350 degrees F for 25 minutes.

VARIATIONS: Top your pie with two packages (8 ounces each) refrigerated biscuits instead of piecrust; use chicken, pork, or lamb instead of beef; sprinkle with grated Parmesan cheese for extra flavor.

*For decoration, cut shapes from the pie dough and place them on the pie.

desserts

Barbara Murphy's Fresh Apple Cake

2	cups sugar
3	cups all-purpose flour
1	teaspoon baking soda
1/2	teaspoon salt
1/2	teaspoon cinnamon
1	cup vegetable oil
2	eggs
3	cups peeled, chopped apples
2	teaspoons vanilla
1	cup chopped walnuts or pecans (optional)
	Powdered sugar

Preheat oven to 350 degrees F. In a large bowl, mix together sugar, flour, baking soda, salt, and cinnamon. In a separate bowl, mix together oil, eggs, apples, vanilla, and, if desired, nuts. Stir the two mixtures together, pour into prepared Bundt pan, and bake for 55 to 60 minutes. Cool, dust with powdered sugar; freeze. Thaw at room temperature.

Serving Suggestion: This is wonderful with vanilla ice cream or drizzled with caramel sauce—or both!

TIP:

Cut cakes with dental floss to minimize crumbs.

Chocolate Macadamia Pie

1	cup sugar
3	eggs
1/2	cup corn syrup
1/2	cup cocoa
3	tablespoons butter, melted
1	teaspoon vanilla
1/4	teaspoon salt
3/4	cup macadamia nuts
3/4	cup chocolate chips
1	baked 9-inch pie shell
	Whipped cream to taste (optional)
	Chocolate shavings for decoration (optional)

Preheat oven to 325 degrees F. In a large bowl, mix sugar, eggs, corn syrup, cocoa, butter, vanilla, and salt. Stir in nuts and chips. Pour mixture into pie shell. Bake 45 to 50 minutes. Quick cool, then decorate with whipped cream and shavings, if desired. Freeze.

Thaw at room temperature, and serve slightly chilled.

VARIATION: Use peanuts or pecans instead of, or in addition to, macadamia nuts.

week seven

Menu

Main Dishes

Blushing Chicken

Crab Cakes with Lime—Cilantro Sauce

Ham Frittata Regatta

Pasta with Ham and Mango Cream Sauce

Torta Rustica

Desserts

Mango Silk Shakes

Pineapple Bars

shopping list

The following list is exactly what you'll need for the week's dinners, so shop accordingly.
You need only purchase those items you don't already have on hand.

....

**BAKING MIXES
AND FLOURS**

2 teaspoons baking soda

2 cups all-purpose flour

**BREADS AND
GRAINS/PASTA/RICE**

3 cups bread crumbs

I loaf frozen bread dough*

I pound fettuccine

CHEESE/DAIRY/EGGS

1/2 cup grated Cheddar cheese

I package (8 ounces) cream
  cheese

I cup grated mozzarella cheese

1/2 cup freshly grated Parmesan
  cheese

I cup ricotta cheese

1/4 cup (1/2 stick) butter

3 cups premium vanilla ice cream

1/2 cup sour cream

I cup whipping cream

Whipped cream to scoop on
  Mango Silk Shakes

I carton (8 ounces) lime or key
  lime pie-flavored yogurt

13 eggs

CONDIMENTS AND SAUCES

I can (15 ounces) whole cranberry
  sauce

2 tablespoons mayonnaise

3 tablespoons plus 1/3 cup whole-
  grain mustard

1/2 cup bottled pesto sauce

1/4 teaspoon plus 5 drops
  Tabasco sauce

2 tablespoon-cubes frozen white
  sauce, or I tablespoon each
  butter and flour, combined

**FLAVORINGS/HERBS†/
SEASONINGS/SPICES**

2 teaspoons Caribbean Jerk
  Seasoning

I tablespoon fresh cilantro

I teaspoon fennel seeds

1/4 teaspoon garlic powder

Fresh nutmeg to sprinkle on
  Mango Silk Shakes

1/2 teaspoon paprika

2 tablespoons chopped fresh
  parsley

1/2 teaspoon red (cayenne)
  pepper

Salt and pepper

2 teaspoons vanilla

FRUITS/NUTS/VEGETABLES

2 mangos, or 2 cups diced bottled
  mango

I can (20 ounces) crushed pineapple in heavy syrup

1/2 cup crushed macadamia nuts
  (optional, for pineapple bars)

I cup frozen corn (may substitute
  canned)

I small onion

3 cups fresh or frozen chopped
  onion

1/2 cup green bell pepper

I 1/2 cups diced roasted red
  peppers

I package (10 ounces) frozen
  chopped spinach

LIQUIDS

1/2 cup cream of coconut

MEAT/SEAFOOD

4 whole chicken breasts

I 1/2 pounds crab meat (may use
  canned)

I pound cooked ham

I pound thinly sliced deli ham

OILS

2 tablespoons plus 3/4 cup
  olive oil

I tablespoon vegetable oil

**SWEETS AND
SWEETENERS**

1/4 cup brown sugar

I 3/4 pounds powdered sugar

I 1/2 cups sugar

*You can substitute pastry for two piecrusts for one of the frozen loaves of bread dough.

†If using fresh herbs, double the amount listed here.

PUTTING IT ALL TOGETHER

1. Thaw bread dough and/or pastry, onions, spinach, and corn. Soften cream cheese. Thaw 2 tablespoon-cubes frozen white sauce mix, or mix together 1 tablespoon each butter and flour.

2. In a large skillet, sauté frozen chopped onion in 2 tablespoons olive oil.

3. Squeeze thawed spinach dry.

4. Dice 1 pound of cooked ham, green bell pepper, and 1/2 cup of roasted red peppers.

5. Chop parsley and cilantro.

6. Mince small onion.

7. Dice mango.

8. Grate cheese (if not already grated).

9. Make crab cake mixture and start it chilling.

10. Grease a 9-inch springform pan, an 11 × 17-inch jelly roll pan, and a 9 × 13-inch baking dish.

TIP:
Place your cutting board on a damp dish towel to prevent sliding as you're chopping and cutting.

Using everything you have just prepared, create these simple, tasty dishes.

Main Dishes

Blushing Chicken

4	whole chicken breasts
1	can (15 ounces) whole cranberry sauce
1/4	cup brown sugar
3	tablespoons whole-grain mustard
1/2	teaspoon paprika
1/4	teaspoon garlic powder
1/4	teaspoon red (cayenne) pepper

Preheat oven to 350 degrees F. Place chicken breasts in prepared 9 × 13-inch baking dish. In a medium bowl, mix cranberry sauce, brown sugar, mustard, paprika, garlic powder, and pepper. Brush half of this glaze over chicken. Bake for 35 minutes. Brush remaining glaze over chicken. Bake for 10 more minutes. Quick cool and freeze.

When ready to serve, wrap in foil and reheat in the oven at 350 degrees F for 20 minutes.

Serving Suggestion: *Delicious with rice and steamed green beans!*

NOTE: There's something wonderful about the combination of cranberries and poultry. Don't wait until Thanksgiving to enjoy them.

Crab Cakes with
Lime–Cilantro Sauce

1 1/2	pounds crab meat
3	cups bread crumbs
1	small onion, minced
3	eggs
2	tablespoons mayonnaise
1/4	teaspoon red (cayenne) pepper
1/4	teaspoon ground black pepper
1/4	teaspoon Tabasco sauce
3/4	cup olive oil
1	carton (8 ounces) lime or key lime pie-flavored yogurt
1/2	cup sour cream
1/3	cup whole-grain mustard
1	tablespoon chopped fresh cilantro

In a large bowl, combine crab meat, bread crumbs, onion, eggs, mayonnaise, peppers, and Tabasco sauce. Chill mixture for 20 minutes. Form into 12 crab cakes. In a large skillet over medium heat, sauté crab cakes in oil until golden, about 5 minutes per side. Quick cool and freeze.

Stir remaining ingredients in a small saucepan over low heat until well mixed. Freeze in separate container.

When ready to serve, warm crab cakes in oven or microwave (wrap in paper towels and microwave for 4 minutes or bake, covered, in standard oven at 300 degrees F for 10 to 12 minutes. Heat lime–cilantro sauce in a small saucepan. Drizzle over hot crab cakes.

VARIATIONS: Use tangerine or lemon yogurt instead of lime. Try this recipe with flaked salmon; couscous instead of bread crumbs; pesto instead of mayonnaise; dill instead of cilantro; a coating of crushed pine nuts.

Serving Suggestion: These are excellent with stir-fried vegetables. Mango Silk Shakes (page 145) make a great dessert with this dish.

Ham Frittata Regatta

1/2	cup chopped green bell pepper
1	tablespoon vegetable or olive oil
1	pound diced cooked ham
1	cup frozen corn, thawed, or canned corn, drained
1/2	cup diced roasted red peppers
1/2	cup sautéed chopped onion
6	eggs
2	tablespoons chopped fresh parsley
5	drops Tabasco sauce
	Salt and pepper to taste
1/2	cup grated Cheddar cheese

In large skillet over medium heat, sauté green bell pepper in oil until tender. Add ham, corn, red peppers, and onion.

In a medium bowl, whisk eggs with parsley, Tabasco, salt, and pepper. Divide ham mixture among four serving dishes. Pour egg mixture over ham. Microwave on high for 2 minutes, then top with cheese. Slip under broiler for another 2 minutes to brown.

Quick cool, then freeze.

When ready to serve, warm in oven at 350 degrees F for 20 minutes.

VARIATION: Oval, ovenproof side dishes can turn this colorful Italian omelet into individual servings. When I created this recipe, I made individual ones in boat-shaped ramekins (or dishes). They reminded me of a boat race, or regatta, all of the dishes sailing down the table. You can even stick a corner of cracker bread in the center to make a sail. You can also broil the entire recipe in an ovenproof skillet, and slice cooked frittata into wedges. To cook in skillet, leave ham mixture in skillet and pour eggs over all. Cook without stirring until edges turn tan. When firm, sprinkle with cheese, then slide under broiler for 2 minutes to brown. Freeze as directed above.

Pasta with Ham and Mango Cream Sauce

1	pound fettuccine
1	cup whipping cream
2	tablespoon-cubes frozen white sauce, thawed, or 1 table-spoon each butter and flour, combined
1	mango, peeled, pitted, diced, drained, and patted dry, or 1 cup bottled diced mango
2	teaspoons Caribbean Jerk Seasoning
1/2	pound sliced ham, cut into 1/2-inch strips
	Freshly grated Parmesan cheese

In a large pot of water, cook fettuccine until *al dente*, then drain. While pasta cooks, prepare sauce.

In a medium saucepan, simmer and stir whipping cream, white sauce cubes or flour and butter, mango, and Jerk seasoning until sauce begins to thicken, about 10 minutes.

Stir in ham. Pour mixture over cooked pasta, quick chill, and freeze in resealable bags.

When ready to eat, thaw in refrigerator, then warm in saucepan, adding milk if necessary. Serve sprinkled with fresh Parmesan.

VARIATION: Use crushed pineapple in place of the mango.

Most households have a tall green shaker of Parmesan cheese in their pantries for spaghetti night. This is so different from freshly grated Parmesan, it's like comparing powdered milk to ice cream. Please invest the extra few cents in freshly grated Parmesan. You can buy it in plastic tubs or grate it yourself, and it makes all the difference in the world. (You'll start sprinkling it into soups and salads, too.)

Torta Rustica

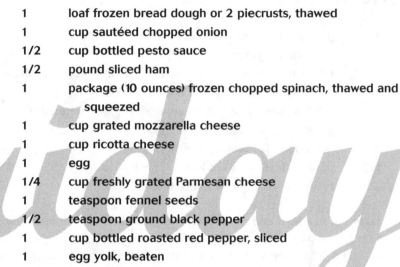

1	loaf frozen bread dough or 2 piecrusts, thawed
1	cup sautéed chopped onion
1/2	cup bottled pesto sauce
1/2	pound sliced ham
1	package (10 ounces) frozen chopped spinach, thawed and squeezed
1	cup grated mozzarella cheese
1	cup ricotta cheese
1	egg
1/4	cup freshly grated Parmesan cheese
1	teaspoon fennel seeds
1/2	teaspoon ground black pepper
1	cup bottled roasted red pepper, sliced
1	egg yolk, beaten

On a floured surface, roll out dough to form a 9-inch circle and a 15-inch circle. Place larger circle in 9-inch greased springform pan, over bottom and halfway up sides. Reserve smaller circle for top.

Preheat oven to 350 degrees F. In a small bowl, mix onion with pesto and spread half of mixture over bottom of crust. Cover with half the ham slices.

In a large bowl, mix spinach, mozzarella, ricotta, egg, Parmesan, fennel, and black pepper. Spread half of this mixture over ham.

Top with half the sliced peppers. Repeat layers: onion, ham, spinach, peppers. Top with 9-inch dough. Pinch dough edges to seal top and bottom. Vent with a fork, or decorate with pastry cutouts. Brush with beaten yolk. Bake on lowest rack in oven for 1 hour. Quick cool, then remove from pan. Wrap tightly in foil and freeze.

To serve, thaw overnight in refrigerator, and bake at 350 degrees F, wrapped in foil, for 50 minutes.

Desserts

Mango Silk Shakes

1	mango, peeled and pitted or 1 cup bottled mango, diced
1/2	cup cream of coconut
3	cups vanilla ice cream
	Whipped cream
	Freshly ground nutmeg

Purée mango in blender. Add cream of coconut. Whirl in ice cream. Put in freezer to serve later, or serve in chilled goblets with a scoop of whipped cream and a sprinkling of ground nutmeg on top.

VARIATION: Try pineapple, cherries, or papaya in place of mango.

Presentation really does make a difference. A relatively simple ice cream becomes more of a dessert when served in a chilled goblet than if simply scooped into a morning cereal bowl.

Pineapple Bars

2	cups all-purpose flour
1 1/2	cups sugar
2	teaspoons baking soda
1	can (20 ounces) crushed pineapple in heavy syrup
2	eggs, beaten
2	teaspoons vanilla
1 3/4	pounds powdered sugar
1	package (8 ounces) cream cheese, softened
1/4	cup butter
1/2	cup crushed macadamia nuts (optional)

Preheat oven to 350 degrees F. In a large bowl, mix flour, sugar, and soda. Add pineapple and syrup, eggs, and half the vanilla. Mix well. Pour into greased 11 × 17-inch jelly roll pan and bake for 25 minutes.

While bars bake, in a large bowl mix powdered sugar, cream cheese, butter, the remaining vanilla, and, if desired, nuts. Spread over hot bars as soon as you remove them from the oven. Quick cool, cut into bars, and freeze in an airtight container. When ready to serve, thaw at room temperature.

week eight

Main Dishes
Corn and Crab Stuffed Peppers

Jambalaya Pizza

King Neptune's Chili

Seafood Avalanche Paella

Seafood Quiche

Desserts
Key Lime Ginger Cheesecake

Stickety Doo Dah Ring

Strawberry White Chocolate Cookies

shopping list

The following list is exactly what you'll need for the week's dinners, so shop accordingly. You need only purchase those items you don't already have on hand.

....

BAKING MIXES AND FLOURS

2 1/3 cups buttermilk baking mix
3 tablespoons all-purpose flour

BREADS AND GRAINS/PASTA/RICE

2 cans refrigerator biscuits
1 store-bought pizza crust
2 cups uncooked small-shell pasta
6 ounces uncooked yellow rice

CHEESE/DAIRY/EGGS

2 1/2 cups grated Cheddar cheese
3 packages (8 ounces each) cream cheese
1/2 pound Monterey Jack or jalapeño Jack cheese
2 cups grated mozzarella cheese
1 1/4 cup plus 1 tablespoon butter
18 ounces evaporated milk
Sour cream (optional, for King Neptune's Chili)
Whipped cream (optional, for Key Lime Ginger Cheesecake)
14 eggs

CONDIMENTS AND SAUCES

6 drops Tabasco sauce
1 bottle (15 ounces) tomato salsa

FLAVORINGS/HERBS*/ SEASONINGS/SPICES

1 teaspoon dried basil, or 2 teaspoons fresh
1 envelope (1.25 ounces) chili seasoning mix
1 teaspoon cinnamon
1/2 teaspoon dried marjoram
1/2 teaspoon onion powder
1 teaspoon dried oregano
1/2 teaspoon red (cayenne) pepper
Salt and pepper
1 teaspoon dried tarragon
6 drops green food coloring
2 teaspoons strawberry extract
1 teaspoon vanilla

FRUITS/NUTS/VEGETABLES

2 to 4 limes (for 1 teaspoon grated rind, or zest, and optional curls)
1/3 cup lime juice (key lime, if possible)
1 cup pecan halves (optional, for Stickety Doo Dah Ring)
1/2 cup fresh or frozen asparagus tips
1 can (15 ounces) red kidney beans
1 can (4.5 ounces) chopped mild green, chipotle, or jalapeño chilies
3 cups frozen corn (may use canned)
1 teaspoon crushed garlic plus 3 teaspoons minced garlic
1 green onion (optional, for King Neptune's Chili)
6 cups fresh or frozen chopped onions
1 box (10 ounces) frozen petite peas
12 red, green, and yellow bell peppers
1/2 cup bottled roasted red peppers
1 can (16 ounces) stewed tomatoes
1/2 cup sun-dried tomatoes

LIQUIDS

4 cups or 3 cans (14.5 ounces each) fish stock or chicken broth

MEAT/SEAFOOD

2 cups cooked crab meat (may use canned)
1/4 pound cooked ham
1/4 pound oysters and/or shrimp
1/4 pound smoked sausage
1/2 pound sea scallops
3 pounds plus 2 cups uncooked seafood (white fish, shrimp, scallops, crab, mussels, lobster, clams, salmon— your choice)
1/2 pound shrimp

OILS

5 tablespoons olive oil

SWEETS AND SWEETENERS

6 ounces white chocolate or white chocolate chips
1 box gingersnap cookies (for making 2 cups crumbs)
1 teaspoon honey
1 package (3 ounces) *non*-instant butterscotch pudding mix
1 1/2 cups plus 3 tablespoons brown sugar
1 cup, 2 tablespoons, plus 1 teaspoon granulated sugar

If using fresh herbs, double the amount listed here.

PUTTING IT ALL TOGETHER

1. Thaw onions, corn, and peas. Let cream cheese and 1/2 cup butter come to room temperature.

2. Chop 1 green bell pepper.

3. Drain and chop 1/2 cup sun-dried tomatoes.

4. Cook and slice 1/4 pound smoked sausage.

5. Cook and slice 1/4 pound ham.

6. Cook rice for paella.

7. Reserve 1 cup of chopped onion; sauté the rest in a large skillet, in 2 tablespoons olive oil over medium heat.

8. Break chocolate into chunks.

9. Cut Jack cheese into cubes for King Neptune's Chili. Grate remaining cheeses (if not already grated).

10. Remove stem ends and hollow out 6 of the bell peppers. Blanch them in boiling water for 5 minutes. Drain and place upright in a 9 × 13-inch baking dish.

11. Slice 2 1/2 cups pepper strips from remaining peppers (for Seafood Avalanche Paella and Seafood Fajitas), and sauté in 2 tablespoons olive oil in a medium skillet until fork-tender.

12. Butter a 9-inch pie plate or quiche dish, an 8-inch baking dish, and a Bundt pan.

13. Melt 3/4 cup butter.

14. Whirl gingersnaps in blender or food processor to make 2 cups crumbs.

15. Peel and devein shrimp.

Week Eight

Using everything you have just prepared, create these simple, tasty dishes.

main dishes

Corn and Crab Stuffed Peppers

1/2	cup sautéed chopped onion
1	can (4.5 ounces) chopped mild green, chipotle, or jalapeño chilies
3	cups frozen corn, thawed (may use canned)
6	ounces evaporated milk
6	eggs
3	tablespoons all-purpose flour
1	teaspoon salt
1	teaspoon honey
1/2	teaspoon ground black pepper
2	cups cooked crab meat (may use canned and drained)
4 to 6	large bell peppers, stems off, blanched
1/2	cup grated Cheddar cheese

Preheat oven to 350 degrees F. In a large bowl, mix onion, chilies, corn, milk, eggs, flour, salt, honey, and black pepper. Stir in crab meat. Spoon mixture into peppers. Pour any extra filling into a separate, 8-inch buttered baking dish and bake alongside peppers. Bake for 1 hour or until cooked through. Sprinkle with Cheddar cheese and bake another 10 minutes. Quick cool, wrap tightly, and freeze.

When ready to serve, thaw, then bake, uncovered, at 350 degrees for 15 minutes (if frozen, bake for 45 minutes).

VARIATION: Microwave filled peppers in a microwave-safe dish on full power for 15 minutes.

Jambalaya Pizza

2	tablespoons olive oil
1	green bell pepper, chopped
1	cup frozen chopped onion—not sautéed
1/2	cup sun-dried tomatoes, drained and chopped
1	teaspoon dried basil, or 2 teaspoons fresh
1	teaspoon dried oregano
1	teaspoon minced garlic
1/2	teaspoon red (cayenne) pepper
6	drops Tabasco sauce
1/4	pound smoked sausage, cooked and sliced
1/4	pound ham, cooked and sliced
1/4	pound oysters and/or shrimp
2	cups grated mozzarella cheese
1	store-bought pizza crust

In a large skillet over medium heat, in olive oil, sauté bell pepper, onion, tomatoes, basil, oregano, garlic, red pepper, and Tabasco sauce. When onion is soft, add sausage, ham, and seafood. Cook just until shrimp turns pink.

Sprinkle half the cheese onto the pizza crust. With a slotted spoon, place jambalaya mixture on next. Top with remaining cheese. Wrap tightly and freeze, keeping horizontal. When ready to serve, heat pizza in the oven on a baking sheet at 450 degrees F for 12 to 15 minutes, or until cheese is bubbly.

NOTE: If using fresh herbs, remember to double them. When making any pizza, if you want to ensure a crispier crust, put some cheese on first, before the sauces and toppings.

King Neptune's Chili

3	cups fish or chicken stock
1	bottle (15 ounces) tomato salsa
1	can (15 ounces) red kidney beans
1	cup sautéed chopped onion
1	envelope (1.25 ounces) chili seasoning mix
1	teaspoon sugar
1/2	teaspoon dried marjoram
2	cups uncooked small-shell pasta
1/2	pound shrimp, peeled and deveined
1/2	pound sea scallops
1/2	pound jalapeño Monterey Jack cheese, cubed
	Sour cream (optional)
1	green onion, chopped (optional)

In a large soup pot, heat stock, salsa, beans, onion, chili seasoning mix, sugar, and marjoram to boiling. Add pasta and cook 4 minutes. Add seafood and cook until opaque and pasta is *al dente*, about another 5 minutes. Quick cool, and freeze in four portions.

When ready to serve, reheat in saucepan over medium heat. Stir cubed cheese into each serving. Top with sour cream and chopped green onions, if desired.

VARIATION: Use regular Monterey Jack cheese for a milder version.

Serving Suggestion: Try this with some crunchy bread sticks.

Seafood Avalanche Paella

1	tablespoon olive oil
1	tablespoon butter
1/2	cup sautéed chopped onion
1/2	cup sautéed bell pepper, sliced
1	teaspoon crushed garlic
6	ounces cooked yellow rice
1	can (16 ounces) stewed tomatoes
1	cup fish stock or chicken broth
	Salt and pepper to taste
3	pounds uncooked seafood (shrimp, scallops, white fish, mussels, lobster, crab, clams, salmon, your choice— tradition says to leave shrimp and mussels in the shell)
1	box (10 ounces) frozen petite peas, thawed

Preheat oven to 350 degrees F. In large Dutch oven or ovenproof skillet, combine all ingredients except seafood and peas. Bake, covered, for 15 minutes. (Or simmer on stove top, covered, for 20 minutes). Stir in seafood and peas. Bake 10 more minutes, or until all liquid is absorbed and shrimp is pink. Quick cool, and freeze in freezer bags.

When ready to serve, heat in covered baking dish in oven or microwave until heated through, about 15 minutes.

VARIATION: For a non-seafood dish, use ham or chicken instead of seafood.

TIP:

Add a pinch of saffron to white rice to make yellow rice.

Seafood Quiche

2	cups seafood (shrimp, crab, lobster, clams, your choice)
2	cups grated Cheddar cheese
1/2	cup asparagus tips
1/2	cup bottled roasted red peppers, chopped
3	eggs, beaten
1	(12 ounces) can evaporated milk
1	teaspoon dried tarragon
1/2	teaspoon onion powder
	Salt and pepper to taste

Preheat oven to 375 degrees F. In a greased 9-inch pie plate or quiche dish, place seafood, cheese, asparagus tips, and red peppers. In a small bowl, mix eggs, milk, and seasonings. Pour over seafood. Bake 30 minutes. Quick cool, wrap in foil, and freeze.

When ready to serve, leave in foil and warm in oven at 350 degrees F for 25 minutes or until heated through. Garnish with additional red pepper slices.

Serving Suggestion: Serve with fresh seasonal fruit.

desserts

Key Lime Ginger Cheesecake

2	cups gingersnap crumbs
1/4	cup butter, melted
3	tablespoons brown sugar
3	packages (8 ounces) cream cheese, softened
1	cup sugar
4	eggs
1/3	cup lime juice
1	teaspoon vanilla
6	drops green food coloring
1	teaspoon lime zest or grated rind
	Whipped cream (optional)
	Lime curls (optional)

Preheat oven to 325 degrees F. In a medium bowl, stir together ginger-snap crumbs, butter, and brown sugar. Press mixture onto bottom of 10-inch springform pan. Do not bake.

In a large bowl, beat cream cheese and sugar until fluffy. Add eggs, lime juice, vanilla, food coloring, and lime zest. Beat thoroughly. Pour into crust and bake for 50 minutes. Cool. Wrap tightly and freeze.

When ready to serve, thaw at room temperature. Serve cool, topped with whipped cream and lime curls, if desired.

VARIATION: Make it a little sweeter using graham cracker crumbs instead of gingersnap crumbs.

TIP:

If you want to freeze whipping cream, whip it first. Otherwise, it won't whip up as fluffy. Keep frozen in small dollops on waxed paper. (Once the dollops are frozen, transfer them to a rigid container). Thaw 20 minutes when ready to use them.

Stickety Doo Dah Ring

1	cup pecan halves (optional)
1	package (3 ounces) *non*-instant butterscotch pudding mix
3/4	cup packed brown sugar
1	teaspoon cinnamon
2	cans refrigerator biscuits
1/2	cup butter, melted

Place pecan halves, if using, rounded side down, in buttered Bundt pan. In a large resealable plastic bag, combine pudding mix, brown sugar, and cinnamon. Separate biscuits and toss in the mixture until coated. Pour in Bundt pan. Drizzle with melted butter. Cover with plastic wrap and chill overnight.

Bake at 375 degrees F for 30 minutes, then invert rolls onto a serving plate, scraping sauce over all. If you can resist eating them immediately, put them in a freezer container and freeze.

When ready to serve, thaw at room temperature. Heat, covered, in microwave for 2 minutes or in oven for 8 minutes at 300 degrees F.

TIP:

Plastic wrap will adhere tightly if you moisten the sides of your bowl.

Strawberry White Chocolate Cookies

1/2	cup butter, softened
3/4	cup packed brown sugar
2	tablespoons granulated sugar
1	egg
2	teaspoons strawberry extract
2 1/3	cups buttermilk baking mix
6	ounces white chocolate, broken into chunks
	(or white chocolate chips)

Preheat oven to 350 degrees F. In a large bowl, beat butter, sugars, egg, and extract until fluffy. Stir in baking mix and white chocolate. Drop teaspoons of dough onto an ungreased baking sheet. Bake 8 to 10 minutes; do not brown. Cool 1 minute, then transfer cookies from baking sheet to wire rack. Makes about 3 dozen cookies. Freeze in lidded freezer container.

VARIATION: Use any extract flavor—not just strawberry.

week nine

Menu

Main Dishes

Is It Hot in Here or Is It This Soup?

Indonesian Pork

Italian Lover Sandwiches

Pork Chops with Chili–Apricot Sauce

Spinach-Stuffed Manicotti

Side Dish

Cheesy Spinach Loaf

Desserts

Lemon Pound Cake

Plantation Pecan Ball Candy

shopping list

The following list is exactly what you'll need for the week's dinners, so shop accordingly. You need only purchase those items you don't already have on hand.

BAKING MIXES AND FLOURS
1/2 cup all-purpose flour
3 cups cake flour

BREADS AND GRAINS/PASTA/RICE
4 (6-inch) submarine sandwich rolls
12 (8 ounces) manicotti pasta noodles
3/4 cup uncooked rice (1 1/2 cups cooked rice)

CHEESE/DAIRY/EGGS
2 cups grated Cheddar cheese
1 package (8 ounces) cream cheese
1 1/2 pound grated mozzarella cheese
8 slices mozzarella cheese
1 container (16 ounces) ricotta cheese
3 sticks butter
1/4 cup milk
1 can (12 ounces) sweetened, condensed milk
1/2 cup sour cream (optional, for soup)
7 eggs

CONDIMENTS AND SAUCES
1 cup peanut butter
2/3 cup bottled pesto sauce
1 jar (26 ounces) tomato-based pasta sauce
1 jar (12 ounces) tomato salsa
1/4 cup soy sauce
1 teaspoon Tabasco sauce
1/2 cup tomato chili sauce
1 tablespoon Worcestershire sauce

FLAVORINGS/HERBS*/ SEASONINGS/SPICES
2 tablespoons horseradish
1 tablespoon garlic powder
1 tablespoon ground ginger
1/2 teaspoon red pepper flakes
Salt and pepper
1 teaspoon lemon extract
1/2 teaspoon orange extract
2 teaspoons vanilla

FRUITS/NUTS/VEGETABLES
4 lemons (for juice and zest)
3 3/4 cups chopped pecans
1/2 cup pine nuts
1 can (15 ounces) black beans
2 teaspoons minced garlic
3 cups fresh or frozen chopped onion
1/2 green bell pepper
1 can (4.5) ounces diced jalapeño peppers (or chopped mild green chilies)
1 jar (16 ounces) roasted red peppers
5 packages (10 ounces) frozen chopped spinach
1 zucchini

LIQUIDS
6 cups tomato juice

MEAT/SEAFOOD
1 pound thinly sliced deli ham
7 pork loin chops, 1-inch thick
1 pound Italian sausage

OILS
1 tablespoon olive oil

SWEETS AND SWEETENERS
1 box (12 ounces) vanilla wafers
1/3 cup apricot jam
3 cups plus 2 teaspoons sugar
1 cup powdered sugar

*If using fresh herbs, double the amount listed here.

PUTTING IT ALL TOGETHER

1. Thaw spinach and onions. Sauté onions in olive oil in a large skillet over medium heat.

2. Allow butter and cream cheese to come to room temperature.

3. Dice and sauté 1/2 green bell pepper.

4. Dice Italian sausage.

5. Cut 3 of the pork chops into strips (for Indonesian Pork).

6. Halve and slice zucchini.

7. Finely crush vanilla wafers in food processor or blender.

8. Crush pecans.

9. Cook rice.

10. Grate cheese (if not already grated).

11. Butter a bread loaf pan or small casserole. Grease Bundt pan.

12. Slice roasted red peppers.

Week Nine

163

Using everything you have just prepared, create these simple, tasty dishes.

main dishes

Is It Hot in Here or Is It This Soup?

1	can (15 ounces) black beans
1/2	green bell pepper, diced and sautéed
1/2	cup sautéed chopped onion
1	can (4.5 ounces) diced jalapeño peppers
1	jar (12 ounces) tomato salsa
6	cups tomato juice
1/2	teaspoon red pepper flakes
1	pound Italian sausage, diced
1	zucchini, halved and sliced
1/2	cup sour cream (optional)

In a large soup pot, combine beans, bell pepper, onion, jalapeños, salsa, tomato juice, and red pepper flakes over medium heat. When boiling, add sausage and zucchini; cook until sausage is no longer pink. Freeze.

When ready to serve, heat in soup pot over medium heat. Top each serving with sour cream, if desired.

VARIATION: Use chopped mild green chilies for a less fiery version.

Serving Suggestion: Cool the fire in this spicy soup by serving it with bread slathered with a mixture of cream cheese and ranch dressing. Follow with a cool fruit sherbet for dessert.

Indonesian Pork

3	pork loin chops, cut into strips
1	cup sautéed chopped onion
1	cup peanut butter
1/4	cup soy sauce
1/4	cup milk
1	tablespoon ground ginger
1	tablespoon garlic powder
2	teaspoons sugar
1	teaspoon Tabasco sauce
	Juice of 1 lemon

Place all ingredients in a large resealable freezer bag and freeze.

When ready to serve, empty bag and stir contents in a large skillet over medium-low heat, until pork is no longer pink.

Serving Suggestion: *Serve this with cooked white rice. Coleslaw on the side is a Dutch tradition.*

Italian Lover Sandwiches

4	(6-inch) submarine sandwich rolls, split
2/3	cup bottled pesto sauce
1/2	cup pine nuts
1	jar (16 ounces) roasted red peppers, drained
1	pound thinly sliced deli ham
1/2	pound mozzarella cheese

Heat broiler. Spread bottom halves of rolls with pesto sauce. Sprinkle on pine nuts, then a layer of red peppers. Follow with ham slices, then mozzarella cheese. Broil until cheese is bubbly, about 2 minutes, then place top roll half onto sandwich, pressing to adhere to cheese. Wrap tightly and freeze.

When ready to serve, thaw in refrigerator and enjoy cold, or reheat in oven, wrapped in foil, at 350 degrees F until cheese is warmed through, about 90 seconds.

Keep herb butters in the freezer and thaw as needed to dress up rolls and sandwiches. Mix butter with orange and thyme, basil and garlic, applesauce and cinnamon, or lemon and dill.

Pork Chops with Chili–Apricot Sauce

4	pork loin chops, 1-inch thick
1/2	cup all-purpose flour
	Salt and pepper to taste
1	tablespoon olive oil
1/2	cup tomato chili sauce
1/3	cup apricot jam
1	tablespoon Worcestershire sauce
1	teaspoon minced garlic

Toss chops in a resealable plastic bag with flour, salt, and pepper. Heat oil in a large skillet over medium heat; brown chops on each side about 4 minutes per side. Stir in chili sauce, jam, Worcestershire, and garlic. Reduce heat to low. Cover and simmer for 20 minutes. Turn and baste halfway through cooking time. Quick cool, then freeze.

When ready to serve, heat in covered dish at 325 degrees F for 25 minutes, or until heated through.

Spinach-Stuffed Manicotti

12	(8 ounces) manicotti pasta
1	pound mozzarella cheese, grated
1	package (10 ounces) frozen chopped spinach, drained and squeezed dry
1	container (16 ounces) ricotta cheese
1	egg
1	teaspoon minced garlic
1	jar (26 ounces) tomato-based pasta sauce

In a large pot of boiling water, cook manicotti just until *al dente.*

While manicotti cooks, prepare filling: In a large bowl, mix half the mozzarella, all the spinach, ricotta, egg, and garlic. Stuff mixture into cooked manicotti.

Pour 1/2 cup of the pasta sauce into a 9 × 13-inch baking dish. Place stuffed manicotti on sauce. Cover with remaining sauce and remaining half of mozzarella cheese. Cover tightly and freeze.

When ready to serve, uncover casserole and bake frozen at 350 degrees F for 30 to 35 minutes.

side dish

Cheesy Spinach Loaf

4	packages (10 ounces each) frozen chopped spinach, thawed and drained
2	cups grated Cheddar cheese
1 1/2	cups cooked rice
3	tablespoons butter, melted
1	teaspoon salt
1/4	teaspoon ground black pepper
2	tablespoons horseradish

In a buttered bread loaf pan or small casserole, combine all ingredients. Cover and freeze.

When ready to serve, bake frozen at 350 degrees F for 30 minutes.

desserts

Lemon Pound Cake

3	cups sugar
1 1/4	cups butter, softened
1	package (8 ounces) cream cheese, softened
1	tablespoon lemon juice
2	teaspoons vanilla
1	teaspoon lemon extract
1/2	teaspoon orange extract
1/8	teaspoon salt
6	eggs
3	cups cake all-purpose flour

Glaze

1	cup powdered sugar
1	tablespoon butter, softened
2	teaspoons lemon zest
3	tablespoons lemon juice

Preheat oven to 325 degrees F. In a large bowl, mix sugar, butter, and cream cheese until smooth. Add lemon juice, vanilla, extracts, and salt.

Mix well. Add eggs one at a time, beating after each. Add flour; mix until smooth.

Pour into greased Bundt pan and bake for 1 1/2 hours, or until toothpick tests clean. Cool for 10 minutes, then remove from pan onto wire rack. Wrap and freeze.

When ready to serve, thaw at room temperature (allow at least 1 hour to thaw), then cover with glaze. Prepare glaze by mixing sugar, butter, zest, and juice in a small bowl. Drizzle over cake.

VARIATION: Make a Lime Pound Cake by substituting lime juice for lemon juice, lime extract for lemon extract, and lime zest for lemon zest.

Plantation Pecan Ball Candy

1   box (12 ounces) vanilla wafers, finely crushed
3 3/4   cups finely chopped pecans
1   can (12 ounces) sweetened, condensed milk

In a large bowl, mix all ingredients together. Chill. Using a melon baller or spoon, form mixture into 1-inch balls. They can be eaten immediately, kept in the refrigerator, or frozen in a rigid container in the freezer. Makes about 4 dozen candies.

TIP:
Freeze citrus rinds
and grate while
frozen. Much easier!

CHAPTER SIXTEEN

week ten

Main Dishes

Secret Recipe Clam Chowder

Cheese-Filled Tortellini with Tomato—Clam Sauce

Lemon Pepper Sea Bass with Coconut Cream Sauce

Scallops with Honey—Chili Glaze

Seafood Fajitas with Jamaican Salsa

Desserts

Coconut Ice

Raspberry Bread

shopping list

The following list is exactly what you'll need for the week's dinners, so shop accordingly. You need only purchase those items you don't already have on hand.

BREADS AND GRAINS/PASTA/RICE

2 loaves frozen bread dough

8 (6-inch) flour tortillas

2 packages (12 ounces each) or one 24-ounce bag cheese-filled tortellini

2 cups uncooked rice (or 4 cups cooked)

CHEESE/DAIRY/EGGS

1/2 cup butter

1 1/2 quarts plus 1 cup half-and-half

1 can (14 ounces) sweetened, condensed milk

3/4 cup whipping cream

6 eggs

CONDIMENTS AND SAUCES

2 tablespoons whole-grain mustard

1 tablespoon soy sauce

1 cup and 4 tablespoon-cubes frozen white sauce, or 1/2 cup plus 2 tablespoons each flour and butter, combined

FLAVORINGS/HERBS*/ SEASONINGS/SPICES

2 teaspoons dried basil

2 teaspoons Caribbean Jerk Seasoning

1 teaspoon cinnamon

Pinch of ground cloves

1 teaspoon ground cumin

2 tablespoons lemon pepper seasoning

1 teaspoon white pepper

Salt and pepper

3 drops almond extract

FRUITS/NUTS/VEGETABLES

1 tablespoon lime juice

1 mango (may use bottled, sliced mango)

1 cup crushed pineapple

1/2 cup shredded coconut

1 cup chopped pecans (optional, for Raspberry Bread)

1 carrot

2 tablespoons minced chilies, mild or spicy

3 teaspoons crushed garlic

1/2 cup chopped plus 2 tablespoons minced fresh cilantro

2 1/2 teaspoons minced garlic

1/2 teaspoon fresh ground ginger

3 cups fresh or frozen chopped onion

3 bell peppers (green, red, and yellow if possible)

4 red new potatoes

Snow peas for side dish

2/3 cup bottled, marinated sun-dried tomatoes

LIQUIDS

1 cup canned unsweetened coconut milk

1 cup fish stock or chicken broth

MEAT/SEAFOOD

6 slices bacon

4 cans (6 ounces each) minced clams

1 pound sea bass or other white fish filets

16 large fresh sea scallops

1 pound mixed seafood (fish, crab, scallops, shrimp, your choice)

OILS

3 tablespoons olive oil

SWEETS AND SWEETENERS

1 carton (3 ounces) raspberry gelatin

3 tablespoons honey

1/2 cup brown sugar

1/3 cup plus 1/2 cup sugar

*If using fresh herbs, double the amount listed here.

PUTTING IT ALL TOGETHER

1. Thaw onion, bread dough, tortellini. Thaw 1 cup and 4 tablespoon-cubes frozen white sauce, or mix 1/2 cup plus 2 tablespoons of all-purpose flour and 1/2 cup plus 2 tablespoons of butter into a paste.

2. Cook and chop bacon.

3. Sauté onion in 1 tablespoon olive oil (or use bacon drippings) in large skillet over medium heat.

4. Slice bell peppers into strips to make 2 cups; sauté as you did the chopped onion.

5. Boil or sauté mixed seafood, just until barely opaque.

6. Cook rice.

7. Separate whites and yolks of eggs (use the whites for an egg-white omelet breakfast).

8. Prepare Coconut Ice and freeze.

9. Halve and slice carrot.

10. Dice potatoes and boil them immediately as directed for Secret Recipe Clam Chowder.

11. Grease a 9 × 13-inch baking dish. Cut each bread loaf into 8 pieces, then into quarters to make 64 pieces. Place in greased baking dish.

12. Chop cilantro.

13. Boil water for tortellini.

TIP:
Use a copper bowl for beating egg whites—the whites will whip up fluffier because of the chemical reaction between the copper and the egg whites.

Week Ten

Using everything you have just prepared, create these simple, tasty dishes.

main dishes

Secret Recipe Clam Chowder

1	cup (16 cubes) frozen white sauce, thawed,
	or mix 1/2 cup each butter and all-purpose flour
1 1/2	quarts half-and-half
1/2	cup sautéed chopped onion
2	cans (6 ounces each) minced clams with juice
6	slices bacon, cooked and chopped
1	teaspoon white pepper
4	red new potatoes, diced
1	carrot, halved lengthwise and sliced

In a large stockpot over medium-low heat, stir white sauce cubes or flour and butter mixture and half-and-half until mixture begins to thicken. Add onion, clams, bacon, and white pepper. Quick cool and freeze.

In a separate medium saucepan over high heat, boil potatoes and carrot just until fork-tender. Drain vegetables and store in refrigerator.

When ready to serve, mix potatoes and carrots into soup mixture and heat over simmering water for 5 to 10 minutes in top of a double boiler. If too thick, add milk. Do not boil.

Cheese-Filled Tortellini with Tomato-Clam Sauce

2	packages (12 ounces each) or one 24-ounce bag cheese-filled tortellini, thawed
1	cup fish stock or chicken broth
4	tablespoon-cubes frozen white sauce, thawed, or 2 tablespoons each butter and all-purpose flour, combined
2	cans (6.5 ounces each) minced clams with juice
2/3	cup bottled, marinated sun-dried tomatoes, drained and chopped
1/2	cup chopped fresh cilantro
2	teaspoons crushed garlic
2	teaspoons dried crushed basil
1/2	teaspoon ground black pepper

In a large stockpot, boil tortellini in water until *al dente.* In a small saucepan over medium heat, combine stock, white sauce cubes or flour and butter mixture, clams, tomatoes, cilantro, garlic, basil, and pepper. Cook until sauce thickens. Drain tortellini and place in freezer container. Pour sauce over pasta. Quick cool and freeze.

When ready to serve, thaw in refrigerator, then heat in top of double boiler over simmering water.

Lemon Pepper Sea Bass with Coconut Cream Sauce

1	tablespoon olive oil
1	pound sea bass filets or other white fish
1	tablespoon soy sauce
2	tablespoons lemon pepper seasoning
2	teaspoons minced garlic

Heat broiler. Brush broiler pan with olive oil. Brush filets lightly with soy sauce. Sprinkle with lemon pepper and garlic. Place fish on broiler pan about three inches from broiler for 5 to 6 minutes. Just before fish turns opaque (remember, you will cook it again), remove from heat and quick cool. Prepare coconut cream sauce.

Coconut Cream Sauce

1	cup half-and-half
1	cup canned unsweetened coconut milk
6	egg yolks
1/3	cup sugar

Simmer half-and-half and coconut milk in a medium saucepan. Whisk in egg yolks and sugar. Stir over medium-low heat until slightly thickened, about 4 minutes. Do not boil. Strain, then pour over fish filets. Wrap tightly and freeze.

When ready to serve, thaw in refrigerator, then bake at 375 degrees F for 5 minutes.

Serving Suggestion: This white entree goes well with carrots or squash and saffron or wild rice. For additional color, sprinkle tomato and cucumber slices with balsamic vinegar and serve on the side.

Scallops with Honey–Chili Glaze

3	tablespoons honey
2	tablespoons whole-grain mustard
1	tablespoon lime juice
1	tablespoon olive oil
2	tablespoons minced chilies, mild or spicy
1/2	teaspoon minced garlic
1/2	teaspoon fresh ground ginger
16	large fresh sea scallops
4	cups cooked rice
	Snow peas for side dish

In a large skillet over low heat, combine honey, mustard, lime juice, olive oil, chilies, garlic, and ginger. Place scallops in mixture and heat until scallops are not quite opaque. Remember, you'll be heating them again. Pour mixture into freezer container(s) and freeze.

When ready to serve, place frozen scallop mixture directly in top of double boiler and heat until scallops are opaque. Serve over cooked rice with cooked snow peas on the side.

VARIATION: Add canned, sliced water chestnuts to the snow peas for crunch and interest.

Always be careful handling chilies. Use disposable plastic gloves if you're dealing with the really hot ones. And be sure you don't touch your eyes.

Thursd

Seafood Fajitas with Jamaican Salsa

1	pound cooked seafood (fish, crab, shrimp, scallops, your choice)
2	cups sautéed red, green, and yellow bell pepper strips
1	cup sautéed chopped onion
2	tablespoons minced fresh cilantro
1	teaspoon crushed garlic
1	teaspoon ground cumin
1/4	teaspoon ground black pepper
1	cup crushed pineapple, drained
1	mango, peeled, pitted, and diced, or 1 cup bottled mango, diced
2	teaspoons Caribbean Jerk Seasoning
8	(6-inch) flour tortillas

In a large freezer container, combine seafood, pepper strips, onion, cilantro, garlic, cumin, and black pepper. Toss to coat thoroughly. Freeze.

To make Jamaican Salsa, stir pineapple, mango, and Jerk seasoning in a small saucepan until heated through. Freeze separately from seafood mixture.

When ready to serve, heat seafood mixture on stove top in a medium saucepan. Heat salsa in a small saucepan. Heat tortillas, wrapped in foil, in oven at 350 degrees F for 10 minutes. Spoon seafood filling onto warm tortillas, top with a dollop of salsa, wrap, and serve (2 fajitas per person).

TIP:

Warm tortillas by covering them with paper towels and microwaving them on full power for 15 seconds each. This method is much less greasy than frying.

desserts

Coconut Ice

1	can (14 ounces) sweetened, condensed milk
3/4	cup whipping cream
1/2	cup shredded coconut
3	drops almond extract

Whisk all ingredients together. Pour into plastic container and freeze for 2 hours. Pour into large mixing bowl or blender and beat just until fluffy. Freeze again until solid.

VARIATIONS: Roll ball-shaped scoops in toasted coconut; decorate with sprigs of mint; serve in half a coconut.

Week Ten

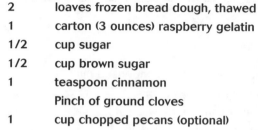

Raspberry Bread

2	loaves frozen bread dough, thawed
1	carton (3 ounces) raspberry gelatin
1/2	cup sugar
1/2	cup brown sugar
1	teaspoon cinnamon
	Pinch of ground cloves
1	cup chopped pecans (optional)
1/2	cup butter, melted

Preheat oven to 350 degrees F. Cut each bread loaf into 8 pieces, then quarter them to make 64 pieces. Place in greased 9 × 13-inch baking dish. Mix gelatin, sugars, cinnamon, cloves, and, if desired, nuts. Sprinkle mixture over bread dough. Drizzle with melted butter. Let rise for 30 minutes, then bake for 30 minutes. Invert into airtight freezer container, allowing glaze to thoroughly coat bread. Freeze.

When ready to serve, thaw at room temperature. Cover and warm in microwave or oven, just until heated through (cover with paper towel and cook for 3 minutes in the microwave, or wrap in foil and place in oven for 15 minutes at 350 degrees).

TIP:

Freeze brown sugar to prevent hard lumps.

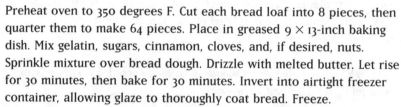

week eleven

Menu

Main Dishes

Tuscany Chicken Soup

Pacific Rim Chicken Salad

Cha-Cha Chicken

Roast Chicken with Yam and Apple Stuffing

Sausage and Sweet Potato Melts

Side Dishes

Cranberry Couscous

Chili Cheese Squares

Poppy Seed Bread

Dessert

Lemon Cookies

shopping list

The following list is exactly what you'll need for the week's dinners, so shop accordingly. You need only purchase those items you don't already have on hand.

....

BAKING MIXES AND FLOURS

2 1/2 teaspoons baking powder

1 lemon cake mix with pudding in the mix

4 1/4 cups all-purpose flour

BREADS AND GRAINS/PASTA/RICE

1 loaf white bread (for making 9 cups soft white bread crumbs)

2/3 cup store-bought bread crumbs

1 package (10 ounces) uncooked couscous

4 (6-inch) sandwich rolls

1 cup ditalini pasta or elbow macaroni

2 packages Asian ramen noodles with seasoning

CHEESE/DAIRY/EGGS

1 1/2 cups grated Colby-Jack cheese

1 pound grated Monterey Jack cheese

3 tablespoons freshly grated Parmesan cheese

2 cups plus 2 tablespoons butter

2 cups cottage cheese

1 1/2 cups milk

1/2 cup sour cream

1 carton (12 ounces) frozen whipped topping

14 eggs

CONDIMENTS AND SAUCES

2 tablespoons tomato paste

6 tablespoons vinegar

FLAVORINGS/HERBS*/ SEASONINGS/SPICES

2 tablespoons chopped fresh herbs (*see Roast Chicken recipe, page 191*)

1/2 teaspoon basil

1/2 teaspoon marjoram

2 tablespoons poppy seeds

1 teaspoon dried rosemary

Salt and pepper

3/4 cup sesame seeds

1 1/2 teaspoons dried thyme

2 teaspoons almond extract

2 teaspoons butter flavoring

2 teaspoons vanilla

FRUITS/NUTS/ VEGETABLES

2 Granny Smith apples (may use other kinds of apples)

2/3 cup dried cranberries

1/2 lemon

1 can (16 ounces) mandarin oranges

1 cup sliced almonds

1 can (15 ounces) black beans

1 can (15 ounces) white beans

1 can (8 ounces) chopped mild green or chipotle chilies

1 teaspoon crushed garlic

1 bunch green onions

1 head romaine lettuce

4 cups fresh or frozen chopped onion

1 can (4 ounces) chopped pimientos

1 can (29 ounces) plus 1 cup sweet potatoes or yams

1 can (15 ounces) stewed tomatoes, Italian style

1 can (6 ounces) sliced water chestnuts

1 zucchini

LIQUIDS

1/2 cup apple juice

2 1/2 cups cranberry-apple juice

5 cups or 4 cans (14.5 ounces each) chicken stock or broth

MEAT/SEAFOOD

6 skinless, boneless chicken half-breasts

10 to 12 assorted chicken parts

1 (4 pound) whole chicken

1 1/2 pounds spicy or mild sausage

OILS

1/4 cup vegetable oil

SWEETS AND SWEETENERS

1 jar (8 ounces) apricot preserves

3 tablespoons maple syrup

3 cups plus 3 tablespoons sugar

1 to 2 cups powdered sugar

*If using fresh herbs, double the amount listed here.

PUTTING IT ALL TOGETHER

1. Thaw onion. Let butter and whipped topping come to room temperature.

2. In a large skillet, cook the sausage until browned and crumbly. Remove sausage with slotted spoon; sauté onions in sausage drippings.

3. Make soft bread crumbs in food processor or blender.

4. Chop herbs.

5. Dice 3 cups of the yams, peel and dice apples; immediately prepare Yam and Apple Stuffing *(see page 192)*.

6. In a large pot of simmering water, cook 6 chicken half-breasts; shred.

7. Toast almonds in dry skillet, just until they begin to brown.

8. Halve and slice the zucchini.

9. Mash the remaining yams.

10. Grease a cookie sheet.

11. Grease 2 loaf pans.

Week Eleven

Using everything you have just prepared, create these simple, tasty dishes.

main dishes

Tuscany Chicken Soup

4	cups chicken stock or broth
2	boneless, skinless, chicken half-breasts, cooked and shredded
1	teaspoon crushed garlic
1/2	teaspoon thyme
1/2	teaspoon marjoram
1/2	teaspoon basil
	Salt and pepper to taste
1	can (15 ounces) stewed tomatoes, Italian style
1	can (15 ounces) white beans, drained
1	cup ditalini pasta or elbow macaroni, cooked and drained
1	zucchini, sliced and halved
	Freshly grated Parmesan cheese

In a large stockpot over medium heat, combine broth, chicken, seasonings, tomatoes, and beans. Bring to a boil. Add pasta and cook for 6 minutes. Add zucchini and cook for another 6 minutes. Quick cool and freeze.

When ready to serve, heat over medium-low heat, and top each serving with freshly grated Parmesan cheese.

Serving Suggestion: Serve this hearty soup with fruit and a selection of cheeses for a complete meal.

Pacific Rim Chicken Salad

2	packages Asian ramen noodles with seasoning
4	skinless, boneless chicken half-breasts, cooked and shredded
1	cup sliced almonds
1	can (16 ounces) mandarin oranges, drained
1	can (6 ounces) sliced water chestnuts
1	cup vegetable oil
3/4	cup sesame seeds
6	tablespoons vinegar
3	tablespoons sugar
1	head romaine lettuce
1	bunch green onions

Break up dry ramen noodles and combine with chicken in a large bowl. Toast almonds in a dry skillet just until they begin to brown. Add to chicken mixture. Toss with oranges and chestnuts.

In a medium bowl, mix ramen seasoning, oil, sesame seeds, vinegar, and sugar. Pour over chicken mixture, tossing to coat. Freeze.

When ready to serve, thaw in refrigerator and toss with lettuce and green onions. And remember, snip the lettuce and onions up with kitchen shears; it's so much easier than using a knife.

Serve cold. Great with Poppy Seed Bread *(see page 196)*.

TIP:

Wrap lettuce in paper towels, then in plastic. Store in the crisper of your refrigerator.

Cha-Cha Chicken

1	jar (8 ounces) apricot preserves
2	tablespoons tomato paste
10 to 12	chicken parts—breasts, thighs, your favorites
2/3	cup store-bought bread crumbs
2/3	cup all-purpose flour
	Reserved spice mixture from Spicy Steaks *(see page 131)*

Preheat oven to 425 degrees F. Mix apricot preserves and tomato paste in a small bowl. Dip chicken pieces into mixture, then toss with crumbs, flour, and spice mixture in a resealable plastic bag until well coated. Place chicken in roasting pan and roast for 35 minutes, or until fork-tender. Quick cool and freeze.

When ready to serve, thaw in refrigerator, then warm in oven for 20 minutes at 350 degrees F.

Serving Suggestion: Great with mashed potatoes and crispy coleslaw. How about a cool sherbet for dessert?

Try baking chicken in a sauce made from a small jar of apricot preserves, half a bottle of Russian dressing, and an envelope of dry onion soup mix. Delicious!

Roast Chicken with Yam and Apple Stuffing

1	whole chicken (4 pounds)
2	tablespoons chopped fresh herbs: rosemary, thyme, basil, tarragon, fennel, sage, or bay leaves (optional)
1/2	lemon
1	cup butter
1	teaspoon salt
1/2	teaspoon pepper

Dark poultry meat near the bones is harmless; oxidation doesn't affect flavor or nutritional value.

Preheat oven to 425 degrees F. Remove giblets from chicken (discard or save for another use), rinse chicken, and wipe inside and out with paper towels. If using herbs, press them under the skin of each chicken breast half. Squeeze and rub half a lemon inside cavity. Rub 1/4 cup of butter inside the cavity, and sprinkle with salt and pepper. Truss or tie legs and wings securely with twine. Place chicken on its side in roasting pan, and rub butter on exposed side. Roast for 20 minutes.

Melt remaining butter. Turn chicken onto other side and brush with melted butter. Roast another 20 minutes. Place bird on its back and baste with pan juices. Roast another 20 minutes. Baste again.

A 4-pound chicken rarely needs to bake for longer than an hour, but if yours is especially meaty it might take another 10 to 15 minutes. When done, it will read 165 degrees F on a meat thermometer, and juices will run close to clear. Use pan drippings to make a sauce or gravy. Spoon in Yam and Apple Stuffing just before serving, or serve stuffing separately.

To freeze and reheat, freeze the stuffing separately in a bag or tight container. Wrap chicken in serving sizes for faster thawing, or as an entire bird, if desired. Thaw the whole chicken for 1 1/2 days in the refrigerator before reheating and serving. Reheat, covered, at 400 degrees for 40 minutes.

(continues)

Yam and Apple Stuffing

1 1/2	pounds cooked spicy or mild sausage
1	cup sautéed chopped onion
2	Granny Smith apples, peeled and diced (may use other apples)
1/2	cup apple juice
1/2	cup butter, melted
1	can (29 ounces) sweet potatoes or yams, drained and diced (3 cups)
9	cups soft white bread crumbs (also try wheat or focaccia bread)
1	cup chicken stock or broth

Preheat oven to 325 degrees F. In a large roasting pan, combine two-thirds of the sausage* with all ingredients and mix thoroughly. Bake, covered, for 20 minutes, then bake, uncovered, for 10 more minutes.

*Remaining sausage will be used for Sausage and Sweet Potato Melts *(see page 193)*.

Sausage and Sweet Potato Melts

1/2	pound spicy or mild sausage, reserved from making stuffing *(see page 192)*
1	can (15 ounces) black beans, drained
1	cup sautéed chopped onions
1	cup sweet potatoes or yams, drained and mashed
1/2	cup sour cream
3	tablespoons maple syrup
4	(6-inch) sandwich rolls, split
1 1/2	cups grated Colby-Jack cheese

Heat broiler. In a large bowl, mix sausage with black beans and onions; set aside. In blender or food processor, whip sweet potatoes or yams, sour cream, and maple syrup until smooth. Spread sweet potato mixture on rolls. Place rolls on baking sheet. Top with sausage mixture, then grated cheese. Slide sandwiches under broiler until cheese is bubbly, 1 to 2 minutes.

VARIATION: Try the sausage and sweet potato mixture on crackers for a delicious appetizer.

TIP:
Stale rolls can be freshened by flashing them under the water faucet, then baking for a minute or two at 400 degrees F.

side dishes

Cranberry Couscous

2 1/2	cups cranberry-apple juice
1	package (10 ounces) uncooked couscous
2/3	cup dried cranberries
2	tablespoons butter
1	teaspoon dried rosemary
1	teaspoon dried thyme
1	teaspoon salt

In a large saucepan over medium-high heat, boil juice. Stir in remaining ingredients, and bring to boil again. Remove from heat, and cover until all liquid is absorbed, about 5 minutes. Fluff and serve. (Or microwave heated juice with couscous for 3 minutes in a covered, microwave-save bowl. Let stand covered for 5 minutes.)

Chili Cheese Squares

1/2	cup butter
10	eggs
1/2	cup all-purpose flour
1	teaspoon baking powder
1	can (8 ounces) chopped mild green or chipotle chilies
2	cups cottage cheese
1	pound grated Monterey Jack cheese
1	can (4 ounces) chopped pimientos

Preheat oven to 400 degrees F. Melt butter in 9 × 13-inch baking dish in oven. In a large bowl, beat eggs lightly, then add flour and baking powder. It will be lumpy. Add melted butter, chilies, cheeses, and pimiento. Stir lightly. Pour into baking dish and bake for 15 minutes. Reduce heat to 350 degrees F and bake for another 30 minutes or until toothpick tests clean. Quick cool and freeze.

When ready to serve, reheat at 350 degrees F for 25 minutes. To serve, slice into squares.

VARIATION: Another option with this delectable dish is to bake each square after it's sliced, to brown on all sides.

Poppy Seed Bread

3	cups all-purpose flour
2 1/4	cups sugar
1 1/2	cups milk
1 1/8	cups vegetable oil
3	eggs
2	tablespoons poppy seeds
1 1/2	teaspoons baking powder
1 1/2	teaspoons vanilla
1 1/2	teaspoons almond extract
1 1/2	teaspoons butter flavoring
1/2	teaspoon salt

Preheat oven to 350 degrees F. In a large bowl, mix all ingredients together and beat at medium speed for 2 minutes. Pour batter into two greased loaf pans. Bake for 45 minutes to 1 hour, or until toothpick tests clean. Pour boiling glaze (recipe follows) over loaves while they're still hot. Cool, then remove from pans. Freeze. When ready to serve, thaw at room temperature.

Almond–Vanilla Glaze for Poppy Seed Bread

1/2	cup sugar
1/4	cup water
1/2	teaspoon vanilla
1/2	teaspoon almond extract
1/2	teaspoon butter flavoring

Mix all ingredients in a small saucepan over moderately high heat until boiling. Pour over poppy seed bread just as bread comes out of oven.

dessert

Lemon Cookies

1	lemon cake mix with pudding in the mix
1	carton (12 ounces) frozen whipped topping, thawed
1	egg
1 to 2	cups powdered sugar

Preheat oven to 350 degrees F. In a large mixing bowl, combine all ingredients except powdered sugar. Make into 1-inch balls and roll in powdered sugar. Place on greased cookie sheet and bake for 15 to 18 minutes. To freeze, wrap cookies tightly in an airtight, rigid container.

VARIATION: Try other cake mix flavors.

Friday

week twelve

Main Dishes

Chipotle Chili Corn Chowder

Bow-Tie Pasta with Pork and Raspberry Cream Sauce

Halibut with Lime Sauce

Presto Pesto Pizza

Tuscany Chili

Dessert

Piña Colada Torte

shopping list

The following list is exactly what you'll need for the week's dinners, so shop accordingly. You need only purchase those items you don't already have on hand.

BREADS AND GRAINS/PASTA/RICE

2 cups crispy rice cereal

1 store-bought pizza crust

1 pound uncooked bow-tie pasta

CHEESE/DAIRY/EGGS

2 cups grated mozzarella cheese

2 tablespoons freshly grated Parmesan cheese

Romano cheese to sprinkle on pasta

9 tablespoons butter

2 cups half-and-half

2 (12 ounces each) cans evaporated milk

3/4 cup whipping cream

CONDIMENTS AND SAUCES

3/4 cup bottled pesto sauce

1 cup store-bought chunky salsa

8 tablespoon-cubes frozen white sauce (or 4 tablespoons each butter and flour, combined)

FLAVORINGS/HERBS*/ SEASONINGS/SPICES

1 tablespoon dried basil

1 tablespoon chili powder

1 tablespoon dried oregano

Salt and pepper

FRUITS/NUTS/VEGETABLES

1/4 cup fresh lime juice

1 carton (10 ounces) frozen raspberries in syrup

1 1/3 cups shredded coconut

1 cup chopped macadamia nuts (optional, for Piña Colada Torte)

2 ounces pine nuts

1 can (15 ounces) white beans

1 tablespoon chopped ancho chilies

1 can (4 ounces) chipotle chilies in adobo sauce

1 cup fresh, frozen, or canned corn

1 can (16 ounces) creamed corn

1 teaspoon crushed garlic

5 cups fresh or frozen chopped onion

1 1/2 cups bottled roasted red peppers

2 cans (15 ounces each) Italian style stewed tomatoes

LIQUIDS

2 cups chicken stock or broth

1 1/2 cups fish stock or water

MEAT/SEAFOOD

16 slices bacon

4 pork chops

1 pound ground sirloin

4 halibut steaks

SWEETS AND SWEETENERS

1/2 cup honey

1 package (6 ounces) white chocolate chips

5 cups (10 ounces) miniature marshmallows

1/2 gallon brick-style pineapple sherbet

*If using fresh herbs, double the amount listed here.

PUTTING IT ALL TOGETHER

1. Cook 4 pork chops in microwave until no longer pink. Slice into thin strips.

2. Thaw white sauce cubes (or mix 1 1/2 tablespoons each of all-purpose flour and butter into a paste), raspberries, corn (if necessary), and onions.

3. Chop and fry bacon in a large skillet. Remove bacon with slotted spoon; sauté onions in drippings.

4. Boil water for bow-tie pasta. Cook pasta for 8 minutes, or *al dente.*

5. Slice roasted red peppers.

6. Chop ancho chilies.

7. In a large skillet, brown and drain pound of ground sirloin.

Leftover French bread can become a bruschetta in no time—just slice it, brush with olive oil, and bake until toasty.

Using everything you have just prepared, create these simple, tasty dishes.

main dishes

Chipotle Chili Corn Chowder

1	cup fresh, frozen, or canned corn
1	can (16 ounces) creamed corn
1	tablespoon chipotle chilies in adobo sauce, chopped
8	slices bacon, chopped and cooked
1/2	cup sautéed chopped onion
2	cups chicken stock or broth
1	can (12 ounces) evaporated milk
2	tablespoon-cubes frozen white sauce, or
	1 tablespoon each butter and all-purpose flour, combined
	Salt and pepper to taste

Combine all ingredients. Freeze in four portions.

When ready to serve, heat, stirring, in top of double boiler until simmering, but do not boil. Be sure to stir until white sauce cubes dissolve and thicken chowder.

VARIATION: For a milder chowder, substitute chopped mild green chilies, or omit the chilies altogether.

Serving Suggestion: *Make this a meal with crusty French bread and your favorite dessert.*

Bow-Tie Pasta with Pork and Raspberry Cream Sauce

6	tablespoon-cubes frozen white sauce, or 3 tablespoons each butter and all-purpose flour, combined
2	cups half-and-half
	Salt and pepper to taste
2	tablespoons freshly grated Parmesan cheese
1	carton (10 ounces) frozen raspberries in syrup, thawed
1/2	cup honey
4	pork chops, previously cooked in microwave and sliced into strips
1	pound bow-tie pasta, cooked and drained

In a medium saucepan over medium heat, whisk white sauce cubes or butter and flour mixture with half-and-half, salt, and pepper. Stir until thickened, about 5 minutes. Stir in cheese, raspberries, and honey.

In a large bowl, toss the raspberry cream sauce, pork strips, and pasta. Freeze in four portions.

When ready to serve, thaw in a covered dish in the oven, or in the top of a double boiler over simmering water for 5 to 10 minutes.

Serve over warm bow-tie pasta.

VARIATION: Omit honey for a less sweet version.

Halibut with Lime Sauce

4	halibut steaks, 1-inch thick
3	tablespoons butter
1 1/2	cups fish stock or water
1	cup sautéed chopped onions
1	cup bottled chunky salsa
1	tablespoon chopped ancho chilies
3/4	cup whipping cream
1/4	cup fresh lime juice

Preheat oven to 400 degrees F. Place halibut steaks in a 9 × 13-inch baking dish. Dot with butter. Pour 1/2 cup of the fish stock or water around steaks. Bake for 15 minutes, or until fish is not quite opaque. (It will finish cooking when you reheat it).

While fish bakes, prepare lime sauce. In a saucepan over medium-low heat, mix onions, salsa, chilies, remaining 1 cup fish stock or water, whipping cream, and lime juice. Simmer, stirring, while fish bakes.

Remove fish from oven and place in rigid freezer container. Pour sauce over fish, cover tightly, and freeze.

When ready to serve, bake fish, covered, at 350 degrees for 25 minutes, or until heated through and fish is opaque.

Presto Pesto Pizza

1/2	cup bottled pesto sauce
1	store-bought pizza crust
1	cup crumbled, cooked bacon (from remaining 8 slices of bacon)
1 1/2	cups bottled roasted red peppers, drained and sliced
2	cups grated mozzarella cheese

Preheat oven to 400 degrees F. Spread pesto sauce over pizza crust. Sprinkle on bacon, then cover with strips of roasted pepper. Mound grated mozzarella on last, and bake until cheese is bubbly, about 8 minutes. Cut into wedges. Wrap each slice tightly and freeze.

When ready to serve, warm the wrapped slices in the oven at 350 degrees F for 15 minutes.

Week Twelve

205

Tuscany Chili

1	pound ground sirloin, browned and drained
1	cup sautéed chopped onion
1	teaspoon crushed garlic
2	cans (15 ounces each) Italian style stewed tomatoes
1	can (15 ounces) white beans
1	tablespoon chili powder
1	tablespoon dried oregano
1	tablespoon dried basil
1/4	cup bottled pesto sauce
	Romano cheese
2	ounces pine nuts

In a large freezer container, mix ground sirloin, onion, garlic, tomatoes, beans, chili powder, oregano, and basil. Freeze.

When ready to serve, pour into large soup pot and simmer until heated through. Top each serving with a spoonful of pesto sauce, a sprinkling of Romano cheese, and pine nuts.

TIP:

Even if the recipe doesn't call for it, always stir a spoonful of sugar into tomato sauces to cut the acidity.

dessert

Piña Colada Torte

1	package (6 ounces) white chocolate chips
1	can (12 ounces) evaporated milk
5	cups (10 ounces) miniature marshmallows
1 1/3	cups shredded coconut
6	tablespoons butter
2	cups crispy rice cereal, crushed
1	cup chopped macadamia nuts (optional)
1/2	gallon brick-style pineapple sherbet

In a small saucepan, heat chips and milk over medium heat to boiling. Stir as it boils gently for 4 minutes. Add marshmallows, stirring until melted. Chill mixture.

In a large skillet over medium-low heat, brown coconut in butter. Add cereal and nuts. Spread 3 cups of this mixture on bottom of a 9 × 13-inch baking dish. Taking small scoops, spoon half the sherbet onto this layer. Cover with half the white chocolate mixture. Repeat layers, ending with a sprinkle of the cereal mixture. Press down firmly. Wrap tightly and freeze.

When ready to serve, remove from freezer 5 to 10 minutes before slicing.

week thirteen

Main Dishes

Angel Hair Pasta and Shrimp with Roasted Red Pepper–Ancho Sauce

Curried Beef and Vegetable Tacos

Ham and Yams in a Jam

Shrimp Polenta

Sweet and Spicy Ham and Fruit Salad

Desserts

Elmer Fudge

Pear Sorbet

shopping list

The following list is exactly what you'll need for the week's dinners, so shop accordingly. You need only purchase those items you don't already have on hand.

BAKING MIXES AND FLOURS

1 cup cornmeal (or instant polenta precooked cornmeal)

1 1/2 tablespoons cornstarch

BREADS AND GRAINS/PASTA/RICE

8 (6-inch) corn tortillas

1 package (12 ounces) angel hair pasta

CHEESE/DAIRY/EGGS

1 cup crumbled goat cheese

1/2 cup freshly grated Parmesan cheese

3/4 cup butter

1 cup cream

1/4 cup milk

1/2 cup sour cream (optional, for tacos)

4 eggs

CONDIMENTS AND SAUCES

1 can (8 ounces) tomato paste

1/4 cup cider vinegar

3 tablespoon-cubes frozen white sauce (or 1 1/2 tablespoons each butter and flour)

1/8 teaspoon Worcestershire sauce

FLAVORINGS/HERBS*/ SEASONINGS/SPICES

1 teaspoon curry powder

3/4 teaspoon minced dry onion

1/8 teaspoon paprika

3/8 teaspoon red (cayenne) pepper

1/2 tablespoon poppy seeds

Salt and pepper

1 tablespoon sesame seeds

1 teaspoon vanilla

FRUITS/NUTS/VEGETABLES

3 Granny Smith apples

1 can (15 ounces) mandarin oranges

2 cans (15 ounces each) pears

1 can (15 ounces) pineapple chunks

1/3 cup raisins

2 cups fresh or frozen strawberries

1/3 cup sliced almonds

1 cup chopped nuts (optional, for Elmer Fudge)

1 avocado

2 dried ancho chilies

1 can (4.5 ounces) diced mild green chilies

1 teaspoon crushed garlic

1 teaspoon minced garlic

1 jar (4.5 ounces) mushrooms

4 cups fresh or frozen chopped onion

1 package (10 ounces) frozen peas and carrots

1 cup bottled roasted red peppers

1 bunch spinach

1 can (16 ounces) yams

LIQUIDS

6 3/4 cups fish or chicken stock or broth

MEAT/SEAFOOD

3 slices bacon

3 pounds cooked ham

1 pound beef rib eye steaks, or your favorite cut

1 1/2 pounds shrimp

OILS

1/4 cup plus 3 tablespoons vegetable oil

SWEETS AND SWEETENERS

1/2 cup unsweetened cocoa

3/4 cup sugar

1 pound plus 1/2 cup powdered sugar

*If using fresh herbs, double the amount listed here.

PUTTING IT ALL TOGETHER

1. Thaw chopped onion, peas and carrots, strawberries if necessary, and 3 tablespoon-cubes frozen white sauce mix, or mix 1 1/2 tablespoons each of all-purpose flour and butter into a paste.

2. Let 1/2 cup butter come to room temperature.

3. Cook the bacon, then sauté onion in bacon drippings.

4. Hard cook the eggs, then peel and quarter them.

5. Cube 3 1/2 cups ham; chop 2 cups ham.

6. Peel and devein shrimp.

7. Chop nuts.

8. Cook and shred beef.

9. Chop roasted red peppers.

10. Rinse, trim, and halve the strawberries.

11. Wash spinach and remove stems.

12. Seed and dice ancho chilies.

13. Freeze canned pears in a plastic container.

14. Butter a 9 × 13-inch baking dish, and grease an 8 × 8-inch microwave-safe dish.

There is one indisputable way to hard cook eggs: Place them in a saucepan of cold water, allowing about an inch of water above the eggs. Heat just to boiling. (Boiled eggs, if done right, are not actually boiled.) Cover and remove from heat. Leave covered for 22 minutes. Remove cover and rinse eggs in cool water. Refrigerate. This is simple chemistry, and the only way to keep the yolks from oxidizing into that unappealing gray-green color.

Using everything you have just prepared, create these simple, tasty dishes.

main dishes

Angel Hair Pasta and Shrimp with Roasted Red Pepper–Ancho Sauce

3	tablespoon-cubes frozen white sauce mix, thawed, or 1 1/2 tablespoons each butter and all-purpose flour, combined
1	cup cream
3/4	cup fish or chicken stock or chicken broth
1/2	pound shrimp, peeled
1	cup bottled roasted red peppers, chopped
1	teaspoon minced garlic
2	dried ancho chilies, seeded and diced
1/2	cup freshly grated Parmesan cheese
12	ounces angel hair pasta

Bring a large soup pot of water to boiling.

While waiting for water to boil, melt white sauce cubes or butter and flour mixture in a large skillet over medium heat, and stir in cream to form thick sauce. Stir in stock or broth, shrimp, roasted red peppers, garlic, ancho chilies, and Parmesan until well mixed. Simmer about 5 minutes, just until shrimp are opaque.

When water in soup pot boils, add angel hair pasta and cook until just *al dente*, stirring to prevent sticking. Drain and place pasta in freezer container(s). Cover with shrimp and sauce.

Wrap tightly. Quick cool and freeze.

When ready to serve, warm in top of double boiler, or bake at 300 degrees F for 20 minutes or until heated through. Do not overbake shrimp.

Curried Beef and Vegetable Tacos

1	pound beef, cooked and shredded
1	cup sautéed chopped onion
1	package (10 ounces) frozen peas and carrots, thawed
1/3	cup raisins
1/3	cup sliced almonds
1	teaspoon crushed garlic
1	teaspoon curry powder
1/8	teaspoon red (cayenne) pepper
3	tablespoons vegetable oil
8	(6-inch) corn tortillas
1	cup crumbled goat cheese
1	avocado, sliced
1/2	cup sour cream (optional)

In a large bowl, mix beef, onion, peas and carrots, raisins, almonds, garlic, curry powder, and red pepper. Seal in plastic bags and freeze.

When ready to serve, heat frozen mixture in an ovenproof bowl for 15 minutes at 350 degrees F.

While beef mixture is heating, heat oil in skillet and fry tortillas in oil just until softened. Drain and pat dry with paper towels. Spoon heated beef mixture into tortillas. Top with goat cheese, sliced avocado, and, if desired, a spoonful of sour cream. Serve 2 tacos per person.

Serve with Elmer Fudge *(see page 217)* for dessert.

Ham and Yams in a Jam

1	can (16 ounces) yams, drained
2	cups chopped ham
3	Granny Smith apples, peeled and sliced
1/2	cup sugar
1 1/2	tablespoons cornstarch
1/2	teaspoon salt
1	cup water
1/4	cup butter

Slice yams and place in 9-inch microwave-safe casserole dish. Stir in chopped ham. Add apples to casserole.

In a small saucepan, stir sugar with cornstarch and salt until thoroughly mixed. Add water and place saucepan over medium-high heat, stirring until sugar dissolves. Stir in butter until it melts. Cook just until boiling, then pour over yam mixture.

Bake in microwave at full power for 20 minutes, or until apples are fork-tender. (Or, bake at 350 degrees F in a standard oven, for 1 hour and 20 minutes.)

Serving Suggestion: Serve over hot, fluffy rice, with steamed greens on the side.

Shrimp Polenta

1	cup cornmeal
6	cups fish or chicken stock
1/2	pound cooked ham, cubed
1	can (8 ounces) tomato paste
1	cup sautéed chopped onion
1	jar (4.5 ounces) mushrooms
1	can (4.5 ounces) diced mild green chilies
3	slices bacon, cooked and crumbled
1/4	teaspoon red (cayenne) pepper
1	pound shrimp, peeled and deveined

Preheat oven to 300 degrees F. In a large saucepan, boil cornmeal in fish stock at medium-high heat. Reduce heat to low and simmer 40 minutes.

In a large bowl, stir together ham, tomato paste, onion, mushrooms, chilies, bacon, and red pepper. Spread half the cornmeal in bottom of buttered 9 × 13-inch baking dish, followed by half of ham mixture, then half of shrimp. Repeat layers. Bake for 20 minutes. Quick cool, wrap tightly, and freeze.

When ready to serve, bake, covered, at 300 degrees F for 20 minutes, or until heated through and shrimp is pink.

Sweet and Spicy Ham and Fruit Salad*

1	bunch spinach, washed and stems removed
4	hard-cooked eggs, peeled and quartered
3	cups cooked ham, cubed
2	cups fresh strawberries, trimmed and halved, or frozen berries, thawed and halved
1	can (15 ounces) mandarin oranges, drained
1	can (15 ounces) pineapple chunks, drained

Place all ingredients in a large salad bowl. Make dressing.

Dressing

1/4	cup sugar
1	tablespoon sesame seeds
1/2	tablespoon poppy seeds
3/4	teaspoon minced dry onion
1/8	teaspoon Worcestershire sauce
1/8	teaspoon paprika
1/4	cup vegetable oil
1/4	cup cider vinegar

Place sugar, sesame seeds, poppy seeds, onion, Worcestershire sauce, and paprika in a food processor or blender fitted with a metal blade (both should be set on medium-high). While running, add oil and vinegar in a slow, steady stream. Blend until thickened. Pour over salad and toss. Or, save dressing in a lidded jar or cruet in the refrigerator.

TIP:
Use salad dressing as a meat marinade; it's great!

*This dish cannot be frozen. All the parts will keep in your refrigerator for the week, and all you have to do is assemble them on the night you want to use them. It makes a marvelous main-dish salad.

desserts

Elmer Fudge

1	pound powdered sugar
1/2	cup unsweetened cocoa
1/2	cup butter, softened
1/4	cup milk
1	teaspoon vanilla
1	cup chopped nuts (optional)

In a large microwave-proof bowl, mix sugar and cocoa. Add butter and milk, but do not stir. Microwave on high for 2 1/2 minutes. Stir well. Add vanilla and, if desired, nuts. Spread in greased 8 × 8-inch dish. Chill fudge before cutting into 1-inch squares. Freeze in airtight container.

VARIATION: Substitute peppermint, orange, or strawberry extract for the vanilla.

Pear Sorbet

2	cans (15 ounces) pears, frozen
1/2	cup powdered sugar

Whip frosty (but not frozen hard) pears with powdered sugar in a blender. Voilà! Instant pear sorbet.

VARIATION: Try this with other fruits, too!

TIP:
Look through
your cupboards for
interesting sorbet
serving cups: tiny
vases, goblets,
or dishes.

Tuesday

week fourteen

Main Dishes

Dijon Chicken Soup

Chicken Asparagus Casserole

Fettuccine with Chicken and Smoked Gouda

Red Snapper with African Salsa

Shanghai Fish

Side Dish

Mama Mia Quick Bread

Desserts

Sweet Orange-Glazed Nuts

Chocolate Chunk Cookies

shopping list

The following list is exactly what you'll need for the week's dinners, so shop accordingly. You need only purchase those items you don't already have on hand.

BAKING MIXES AND FLOURS

2 tablespoons baking powder
1 1/8 teaspoon baking soda
4 1/2 cups all-purpose flour

BREADS AND GRAINS/PASTA/RICE

1 can refrigerated biscuits
1 package (16 ounces) fettuccine
2 1/2 cups oatmeal

CHEESE/DAIRY/EGGS

1 cup grated Cheddar cheese
8 ounces smoked Gouda cheese
1/2 cup grated mozzarella cheese
3/4 cup freshly grated Parmesan cheese
1 1/8 cup butter
1 cup half-and-half
2 cans (13 ounces each) evaporated milk
1/2 cup milk
1 cup sour cream
4 large eggs

CONDIMENTS AND SAUCES

2 teaspoons chicken bouillon granules
1/3 cup Dijon mustard
1/2 cup peanut butter
1/2 cup soy sauce
6 tablespoon-cubes frozen white sauce, or 3 tablespoons each butter and flour, combined

FLAVORINGS/HERBS*/ SEASONINGS/SPICES

1 teaspoon dried basil
1/2 teaspoon fennel seeds
1 teaspoon garlic powder
1 teaspoon dried oregano
1/8 teaspoon red (cayenne) pepper
1/2 teaspoon dried rosemary
Salt and pepper
1/2 teaspoon dried thyme
1 teaspoon vanilla

FRUITS/NUTS/ VEGETABLES

1 banana
1 tablespoon lemon juice
2 oranges plus 3 tablespoons orange juice and 1/2 teaspoon orange zest
1 papaya
1 can (15 ounces) crushed pineapple
3/4 cup shredded coconut
3 1/2 cups nuts (pecans, walnuts, almonds, your choice)
1/2 cup pine nuts (optional, for Mama Mia Quick Bread)
1 package (10 ounces) frozen chopped asparagus, or use 1/2 pound fresh
2 teaspoons crushed garlic
1 cup sliced mushrooms

4 cups fresh or frozen chopped onions
1 red or yellow bell pepper
2 cups bottled roasted red peppers
1 package (10 ounces) frozen chopped spinach

LIQUIDS

1 can (6 ounces) tomato juice

MEAT/SEAFOOD

1/4 pound bacon
11 boneless, skinless split chicken breasts
4 fish filets, about 1 1/2 pounds (snapper, salmon, halibut, roughy, cod, your choice)
1 1/2 pounds red snapper filets

OILS

1/4 cup olive oil

SWEETS AND SWEETENERS

1/2 cup plus 1/3 cup plus 1 tablespoon honey
2 1/2 cups sugar
1 cup brown sugar
16-ounce white chocolate or semisweet chocolate bar

*If using fresh herbs, double the amount listed here.

PUTTING IT ALL TOGETHER

1. Thaw frozen vegetables. Allow butter to come to room temperature.

2. Thaw or prepare white sauce.

3. Cook bacon in large skillet; remove bacon. Sauté frozen chopped onions in drippings.

4. In a large pot of simmering water, cook chicken until no longer pink, about 15 minutes. Drain, cool, and dice (about 11 cups).

5. Dice raw bell pepper.

6. Chop Gouda cheese.

7. Slice 1 cup of the roasted red peppers; dice the other cup.

8. Zest, peel, seed, and chop 2 oranges.

9. Crush pine nuts, if using in Mama Mia Quick Bread *(see page 229)*.

10. Grease two 9 × 13-inch baking dishes and one loaf pan.

11. Break chocolate bar into chunks.

TIP:

Perk up rice or couscous before you freeze it. Stir in a cup of green olives and a dash of curry, cilantro and black beans, chilies and Jack cheese, pecans and thyme, cranberries and orange zest, or a packet of onion soup mix.

Using everything you have just prepared, create these simple, tasty dishes.

main dishes

Dijon Chicken Soup

4	cups cooked, cubed chicken
1	cup sautéed chopped onion
2	cans (13 ounces each) evaporated milk
6	tablespoon-cubes frozen white sauce, thawed, or 3 tablespoons each butter and all-purpose flour, combined
1/3	cup Dijon mustard
2	teaspoons chicken bouillon granules
1/2	teaspoon crushed garlic
1/8	teaspoon red (cayenne) pepper

Combine all ingredients in freezer container(s); freeze.

When ready to serve, thaw overnight in refrigerator. Transfer thawed contents to a large soup pot over medium-low heat. Stir until white sauce cubes melt and soup thickens. Increase heat, if necessary, and thin with regular milk if soup becomes too thick.

Serving Suggestion: *Make this a meal with crusty croutons and a fresh salad.*

Chicken Asparagus Casserole

4	cups cooked, cubed chicken
1	package (10 ounces) frozen chopped asparagus, thawed, or 1/2 pound fresh
1	cup sautéed chopped onion
1	cup sliced mushrooms
1	cup sour cream
1	cup grated Cheddar cheese
1	red or yellow bell pepper, diced
1/2	teaspoon dried rosemary
1/2	teaspoon dried thyme
	Salt and pepper
1	can refrigerated biscuits

In a large bowl, combine chicken, asparagus, onion, mushrooms, sour cream, Cheddar cheese, bell pepper, rosemary, and thyme. Salt and pepper to taste. Pour mixture into a greased 9 × 13-inch baking dish. Top with biscuits; sprinkle biscuits with additional thyme. Wrap tightly and freeze.

When ready to serve, heat frozen casserole, covered, in oven at 350 degrees F for 20 minutes, then uncover and continue baking until biscuits are golden brown, another 10 to 15 minutes.

TIP:

You can still use mushrooms that have begun to wrinkle. Whirl them in a blender, then freeze with a bit of water in ice-cube trays. Next time you need a bit of chopped mushroom for a soup or sauce, you can just drop in a cube or two.

Fettuccine with Chicken and Smoked Gouda

1	package (16 ounces) fettuccine
3	cups cooked, cubed chicken
1	cup bottled roasted red peppers, drained and sliced
1	package (10-ounces) frozen chopped spinach, thawed
1/4	pound bacon, cooked and crumbled
1	cup half-and-half
8	ounces smoked Gouda cheese
1/4	cup freshly grated Parmesan cheese
1	teaspoon crushed garlic

Be adventurous! Use multicolored pastas. Pastas also come in fun shapes.

Cook fettuccine according to package instructions. Drain and place in large bowl. Stir in chicken, red peppers, chopped spinach, and bacon. In a small saucepan over low heat, stir half-and-half, cheeses, and garlic until melted and well blended. Pour over pasta. Quick cool, pour into freezer bags, and freeze.

When ready to serve, heat in top of a double boiler over simmering water. Serve with Mama Mia Quick Bread (*see page 229*).

Red Snapper with African Salsa

1 1/2	pounds red snapper filets
2	tablespoons butter
	Dash of ground black pepper
1	can (15 ounces) crushed pineapple, drained, with juice reserved
2	oranges, peeled, seeded, and chopped
1	banana, chopped
1	papaya, peeled, seeded, and chopped
3/4	cup shredded coconut
1/2	cup peanut butter
1/2	cup honey

Preheat oven to 350 degrees F. Place fish filets in 9 × 13-inch baking dish. Dot with butter and pepper. Pour reserved juice from crushed pineapple around filets. Bake for 10 minutes, or until fish is not quite opaque. Transfer fish to rigid freezer container.

While fish is baking, prepare salsa: In a medium saucepan over medium-low heat, combine remaining ingredients, stirring. Pour salsa over baked filets in freezer container. Wrap tightly and freeze.

When ready to serve, bake, covered, at 350 degrees F for 15 to 20 minutes, or until heated through and fish is opaque.

Shanghai Fish

1/2	cup soy sauce
1/3	cup honey
1	tablespoon lemon juice
1	teaspoon salt
1/2	teaspoon crushed garlic
1/4	teaspoon ground black pepper
4	fish filets, about 1 1/2 pounds (snapper, salmon, halibut, roughy, cod, your choice)

Preheat oven to 350 degrees F. In a small bowl, combine all ingredients except fish. Dip fish into mixture, then place in buttered, 9 × 13-inch baking dish. Pour remaining liquid over fish. Bake 8 to 10 minutes, or until not quite opaque. Wrap tightly and freeze.

When ready to serve, bake fish at 350 degrees F 6 to 7 minutes, or until fish is heated through and opaque.

Serving Suggestion: Serve with steamed vegetables and fried rice.

side dish

Mama Mia Quick Bread

2 1/2	cups all-purpose flour
1	tablespoon baking powder
1/8	teaspoon baking soda
1	teaspoon garlic powder
1	teaspoon dried basil
1	teaspoon dried oregano
1/2	teaspoon fennel seeds
1/2	cup grated mozzarella cheese
1/2	cup freshly grated Parmesan cheese
1	can (6 ounce) tomato juice
1/2	cup milk
2	large eggs
1/4	cup olive oil
1	tablespoon honey
1	cup bottled roasted red peppers, diced
1/2	cup crushed pine nuts (optional)

Preheat oven to 350 degrees F. In a large bowl, mix flour, baking powder, soda, garlic powder, basil, oregano, fennel seeds, mozzarella, and Parmesan.

In a medium bowl, mix tomato juice, milk, eggs, olive oil, and honey, stirring well. Add to dry mixture, then stir in peppers and, if desired, pine nuts. Do not overbeat. Pour batter into a greased loaf pan and bake for 1 hour and 10 minutes. Cool 10 minutes in the pan, then invert onto cooling rack. Wrap tightly and freeze.

When ready to serve, thaw at room temperature.

NOTE: To make a delicious spread for this bread, stir a spoonful of pesto into 1/2 cup butter.

No room for a garden?
Grow herbs on a sunny
windowsill.

desserts

Sweet Orange-Glazed Nuts

1 1/2	cups sugar
1/3	cup water
3	tablespoons orange juice
1/2	teaspoon orange zest
2 1/2	cups nuts (pecans, walnuts, almonds, your choice)

In a medium saucepan over medium heat, stir sugar, water, and orange juice until blended. Stir until mixture reaches the soft ball stage, 240 degrees on a candy thermometer.* Remove from heat and stir in zest and nuts. Pour onto waxed paper and separate. Let harden, then freeze in a rigid freezer container.

VARIATION: Add 1/8 teaspoon red (cayenne) pepper for a sweet and spicy coated nut.

NOTE: These are wonderful served over vanilla ice cream for dessert.

*Soft ball stage means that a small amount of the mixture dropped in ice water forms a soft ball.

The Once-a-Week Cookbook

Chocolate Chunk Cookies

1	cup butter
1	cup sugar
1	cup brown sugar
2	eggs
1	teaspoon vanilla
2 1/2	cups oatmeal
2	cups flour
1	teaspoon baking powder
1	teaspoon baking soda
1/2	teaspoon salt
16	ounces white chocolate or semisweet chocolate bar, broken into chunks
1 1/2	cups nuts (optional)

Preheat oven to 375 degrees F. In a large mixing bowl, beat butter and sugars until creamy. Beat in eggs and vanilla.

In food processor or blender, combine oatmeal, flour, baking powder, baking soda, and salt. Blend into powder. Add to sugar mixture, mixing well. Stir in chocolate and nuts. Roll into 1-inch balls and bake for 6 to 8 minutes, or just until golden. Makes 3 to 4 dozen cookies.

NOTE: Double this recipe if you want to freeze some of the dough for later use.

International Conversion Chart

These are not exact equivalents: they have been slightly rounded to make measuring easier.

LIQUID MEASUREMENTS

American	Imperial	Metric	Australian
2 tablespoons (1 oz.)	1 fl. oz.	30 ml	1 tablespoon
1/4 cup (2 oz.)	2 fl. oz.	60 ml	2 tablespoons
1/3 cup (3 oz.)	3 fl. oz.	80 ml	1/4 cup
1/2 cup (4 oz.)	4 fl. oz.	125 ml	1/3 cup
2/3 cup (5 oz.)	5 fl. oz.	165 ml	1/2 cup
3/4 cup (6 oz.)	6 fl. oz.	185 ml	2/3 cup
1 cup (8 oz.)	8 fl. oz.	250 ml	3/4 cup

SPOON MEASUREMENTS

American	Metric
1/4 teaspoon	1 ml
1/2 teaspoon	2 ml
1 teaspoon	5 ml
1 tablespoon	15 ml

WEIGHTS

US/UK	Metric
1 oz.	30 grams (g)
2 oz.	60 g
4 oz. (1/4 lb)	125 g
5 oz. (1/3 lb)	155 g
6 oz.	185 g
7 oz.	220 g
8 oz. (1/2 lb)	250 g
10 oz.	315 g
12 oz. (3/4 lb)	375 g
14 oz.	440 g
16 oz. (1 lb)	500 g
2 lbs	1 kg

OVEN TEMPERATURES

Farenheit	Centigrade	Gas
250	120	1/2
300	150	2
325	160	3
350	180	4
375	190	5
400	200	6
450	230	8